YOU ARE GOD'S MASTERPIECE.
BY
NONHLANHLA ANNAH THUSI

TO GOD THE FATHER

Thank you for the gift of life, for making me realize the potential in me, for filling my mind with ideas and for the wonderful people you surrounded me with. I have got nothing to pride myself with, but you. Without you I am nothing. I love you Lord.

To my family

I always thank the Lord as I remember you in my prayers, for you have played such a wonderful role in my life. You are special to me.

To my friends

Tsietsi Mashiya: Without you this book is just a pen on paper, thank you for contributing into making the best manuscripts. You are the best.

How can I forget ***Fanie Sefatsa*** who was always willing to give a helpful hand every time I shout in the library. You rock.

To pastor ***JS Mkhwanazi*** thank you, Without you this book is just a dream.

Praise Mangena Maclaishe this book is dedicated to you my friend. Thank you for those encouraging letters, I really appreciated them.

Prologue

"In the beginning the earth was formless and empty; darkness was over the surface of the deep; and the spirit of God was hovering over the waters." Gen1:2

Among the mentioned problems, we notice the greatest problem of them all, "God's spirit is hovering over the waters." The earth was in great chaos to an extent that God's spirit became restless. God needed a vessel that would carry his spirit and prevent it from hovering over the waters. Before he could bring it forth he had to make sure that everything is well prepared, hence He had to clear off the chaotic state the earth was in. He had to prepare for it; for it was about to carry something so dearly to him, "His spirit."

First of all things God created light. Have you ever wondered why light was the first thing to be created? I'm sure this question has never crossed many minds because they read Gen1:2b which says, "Darkness was over the surface of the deep."From there they concluded that God needed light to see where to begin when extricating the complicated earth. That could not be the answer because when reading Psalms 139:11-12 it says darkness is as light to him. So what could be the reason for God to begin his work with light? Let's explore Gen 1:3, 4&5 to find the answer we are searching for. *"And God said, let there be light, and there was light. God saw that light was good and he separated light from the darkness and he called light day and the darkness he called night and there was evening and there was morning – The first day.* From these verses we deduce that God created light so that time can spontaneously be formed. After God has commanded light we see him separating light from darkness calling light day and darkness night, and there was evening there was morning. These four things morning, day, evening and night makes a complete day which indicate time. They on their own represent time.

God is God of time and his work depends on time. If you want to see how organized the person is you can do so by checking the manner in which he uses his time. People who are not working in the speed of time are careless and live in regrets. You hear them with words like, "if I did know better, if I could turn back the hand of time or I wish I did things differently." Why all these regrets? Because they misused their time, forgetting that time lost can never be regained. Ecc3 gives us a concise picture of how important is time. It is present in all our activities and it cannot be excluded in our daily life. I like verse 11 which says *"God made everything beautiful in its time"*. Things which are not done in an appropriate time are abnormal and irritating. Don't be careless, do everything in an appropriate time so that you don't live to regret. Your creator is too organized to be careless, why don't you be like him?

Time makes plans accurate
Without time God would have worked haphazardly, and

it would have been a waste. In his mind he had a plan of how he wanted the universe to be like. For everything to go according to the author's plan they need to be done in appropriate time. That's why the universe is so perfect, there's nothing you can remove or add to it, it stays as it is. People who work without a plan make lots of mistakes. In their work there's always something to correct. Working with such people will be a great disaster because instead of planning a way forward you will be busy correcting their work. They are very good at being confused for they confuse themselves. They always need guidance on a certain matter but once offered they never follow. You hear them with words like;"I don't know what must I do now, should I do this or that." When you point out what should be done they will tell you that your advice sounds good but not really convincing. From there they become stressed again. If you plan ahead your plans will always tell you what to do next.

Again people without plans are very good at making wrong decisions. You will be surprised when finding a young man toiling so much at work to earn a living, but spending all the salary that he gets on liquor with an eye twinkle. The problem is, he doesn't have plans for his salary. So the best thing he can do with it is to liquor it all. If I can be given time to advice such people, I'll advice them to use their money wisely, not on alcohol. There's nothing better about alcohol. For you drink it and pee it all out. Drink and do the same process again and again. Alcohol it is not entertaining but it turns you into a harebrained person. The point I'm trying to make here is "plan ahead for anything that is not planned is in vain." A sage has ever said, "If you fail to plan, you plan to fail. A person who fails to plan for his salary is worse than the one who is not working. Teenagers who failed to plan for their lives find themselves being single mothers before the right time. When they get married their children will be forced to be fathered by men whom are not their really fathers. The reality will always state that they might be calling them dads but they are not their flesh and blood. A plan limits your freedom and makes you courteous when it comes to time. Use your time wise, for it is the only treasure that leads to great opportunities if well used. If God hadn't worked according to plan and time the universe wouldn't be so perfect.

The second day God commanded the expanse between the waters. His spirit has hovered enough in a space where there is no direction. When reading this, one should learn that God has direction. So as His images we must have direction. We must avoid working randomly as though we don't want to finish. Work without direction is unending. Direction allows you to have a starting and an ending point. Which means you can see the end in the beginning. That will encourage you to keep moving no matter how far you are to the end so that you leave a conspicuous mark wherever you have laid your hand or set your foot.

The third day God commanded water under the sky to gather in one place and dry ground to appear. Here we see God extricating the land so that his direction becomes clear. The lesson we need to take here is; before we can begin our work we need to gather up resources in one place so that we save time and keep the environment we are going to use clean. At this stage God would have brought forth His vessel but He decided not to. Not because He had all time to Himself, but the universe was not yet in the way He intended. With water gathered up the land was an empty space. Now God commanded the land to produce vegetation and all various plants.

On the fourth day God commanded lights in the expanse to separate day and night. They were also going to serve as signs to mark seasons days and years, and to give light to the earth. One might ask this question, "Why was God decorating the earth in such order? The answer is simple, because there was a special thing on the way. Take the society you live in as an example, if they can say the president or anybody special is visiting. The municipality will go out of its way to prepare for that special body. The infrastructures will rapidly take place. The streets and the place for his arrival will be well cleaned just to impress that coming visitor. Take your home as another example, when there's a coming visitor the house will be turned upside down just to clean it. I'm sure you now understand where we have inherited this character.

The fifth day God created all different creatures and the birds. They were instructed how to live and move. The bird were instructed to fly in the expanse of the sky across the ground, other creatures were instructed to teem with water, life stock and wild animals to move on the ground. And there after he blessed them and said be fruitful and increase in number. God is an intelligent mastermind whom you can trust to guide your life.

Each day ended with God approving his work, seeing everything he has created; good. In everything he created he patted himself on the shoulder for the job well done. Let's check what the sixth day of creation has got for us: for the first time in the whole creation we hear God discussing with the heavenly host. In everything he created he just commanded and it came to pass. He said the word and the array of things were the results. Now when it came to his special vessel that was going to carry his spirit there was no command but discussion. In the discussion he mentioned how he wanted the vessel to look like and its duties were also mentioned. For the first time in creation we see God forming something by himself. It has always been the word and everything obeying the given commandment. For the first time we see God breathing in what he has created. "The Lord God formed man from dust of the ground and breathed in his nostrils the breath of life, and man became a living being." Gen2:7

In all the things God created man is the only creature that contains his spirit, carries his image and likeness, and that has the authority over the earth. In all that he created the Lord saw them good but when it came to man things changed from good to very good. Meaning eventually I have my MASTERPIECE.

On the seventh day God rested from all his work, not because he was tired but for the fact that the universe was complete and most of them all he got what he longed for and was satisfied. Take yourself for an example, if there is something that you really need you do not rest until it is found. Once it is found you sigh with relief that you have found it and all the searches comes to a halt. With man on earth God's joy was complete. Have you noticed in marriages where there are no children there is no satisfaction? Even if there is something that can bring the couple joy the thought that only if we had the child of our own snatches that joy away. Dissatisfaction causes unending complains that consumes all the peace and leave the marriage as the wilderness. But once the child is born the couples leave in the jubilee. Everything that belongs to them will be under the child's name before he can even pronounce the first word. That's what God did and is still doing to this day. Before man was created God put everything under his dominion. "Then God said, let us make man in our own image, in our own likeness and let them rule over the fish of the sea, over the life stock, over all the earth and over the creatures that moves along the ground." Note, "Here man was not yet formed, God was visualizing the future of what He was about to create that it will rule His work.

Nevertheless man was the image of God predestined to rule, his dominion was limited as far as the earth only, leaving God in charge of the heavens. God has also predestined you and I to be the best in this life, but only in our fields. Before you were conceived God said, let us create a pilot, a doctor, an artist, etc. Jeremiah is not the only one whom God knew and appointed before birth Jer1:4-5. You are also appointed by God in a certain field which you will never know until you are there or ask God.

Do not be afraid, you are God with a small g whereas he is God with a capital G, Ps82:1-6. When you criticize your self you are also criticizing the intelligence of the one who created you, Rom14:7-8. No matter the circumstances; you were created to outshine; never underestimate you abilities. You are the most outstanding piece among
all God's work. If he were to make a show off you would be his showpiece. Keep shining!!!

Chapter 1

Never miss you identity.

"Moses said to God, suppose I go to the Israelites and say to them, the God of your fathers has sent me to you, and they ask me, what is his name? Then what shall I tell them? God said to Moses I AM WHO I AM. This is what you are to say to the Israelites I AM has sent me to you." Ex3:13-14

Who are you?

Children from lower grades at school are taught to sing these words, "I am unique and special." These words became a popular song to many but their meaning remained elusive. The purpose of teaching young minds such words was to ensure that they grow up knowing that within every one of them there is a character that is "without equal, distinguished and excelling others of its kind." This character is not found only in few of us but in each and every person that still has breath in his nostrils. Teachers knew that there are circumstances that hamper one's way to an extent that you don't notice whether you are moving forward or backward, but the person who has captured the meaning of "I am unique and special" will make it through. Even in hard circumstances whereby people swears that no one can make it through he who knows himself, he who is aware of the hidden ability within himself will make it through and leave everyone surprised. Besides the circumstances that hamper your way, there are people out there with untamed tongues. People whom are very good at saying negative things so that their fellow brothers lose focus. It's like they were carefully chosen and trained to excel in their department of hindering people from discovering themselves. Let me whisper this in your ears, in life you will never win any battle unless you discover yourself. Poverty it's in the minds of those who haven't discovered themselves.

A person who has discovered and knows himself doesn't allow people or circumstances to tell his identity/character. He overlooks a curse or insult and move on for there's future to prepare for. He doesn't comply with every negative thrown his way but he believes in God. He doesn't focus on temporary conditions instead he visualizes the future. Instead of worrying about his future he plans it and tells it what to have in store for him. In all circumstances he is like God. When God spoke to Moses in the scripture read it is quite clear that the Israelites knew him not. The situation was not allowing him to identify himself as I AM yet he did. Imagine going to people saying I AM sent me to you. What will those people think of you? They will definitely take you for a fool. It sounds so ridiculous doesn't it? That's how people with their identities sounds. In a shack of one room they dream about having a mansion, not just a mansion but a very huge one. God knew that the Israelites knew him not, even Moses himself didn't but he didn't compromise his identity. He said go and tell them that I AM has sent you.

Identity allows you to understand yourself and never pay attention to those who don't because no one knows you better than yourself. It's either they understand you or leave you alone. The person who can best identify himself is not afraid of challenges, and he is always ready to take the first step. He speaks with authority and everyone gives attention. Other people's objectives are not a threat to him. Let's speak a little about David: David defeated Goliath before he could even engage in a fight with him. Why? Because he knew himself and the God that he serves. He went to war with victory in his mind. That's how we defeat wars. We start fighting them first in our minds by the time we get into the battle field we have already won before we can even start fighting.

In the story of David we meet two people who knew themselves, Sam17:4. David knew himself because once he saw Goliath he wanted to tackle him and Goliath also knew himself because he was defying God's armies asking for a man who can fight him. The rule that applies here is, "never underestimate your opponent." For forty days and forty nights this champion despised Israel but no one took his stand against him until David said, "it is enough, not anymore Goliath, I am going to silence you once and forever."

Let's look at what the person who can't identify himself does. David's brother burned with anger when hearing David inquiring about the philistine. He doesn't know himself; now he becomes a stumbling block to the one who does. You know why they couldn't fight Goliath? Because they knew that he was a champion; yet failed to understand that they are God's army and God can never be defeated. Saul the king tried to discourage David by pointing out the reputation Goliath has. He told David that Goliath has fought men since from his youth, but still this young man who knew himself wouldn't shrink back because he had a testimony too.(David was a sheep tender and he once killed the lion and the bear that tried to kill his father's flock). So who was Goliath compared to David? "He was one of them." Never be afraid of a person's reputation better be afraid of his character.

A positive identity it is built by the character that is possessed. The two works hand in hand and they can't be separated.

Before I may proceed, let me explain this, there is character and there is reputation. The former words are different. Reputation is how people think about you according to what they know, and character is how God thinks about you. For instance people might see the way you are dressed and conclude that you are nobody, whereas God sees somebody in you. Here, the choice is yours, you can choose to activate God's thought and become somebody or you can choose to activate people's ideas and become nobody. The bible describes Gideon coming from the weakest clan in Manasseh and being the least in his family, Judges6:12. That was his reputation. Let's focus on his character, what God thinks about him, "a mighty warrior." Has Gideon fought any battle? NO! He was even hiding from the battle. Why God called him mighty warrior? Because He is the only one who best knows us.

If God calls Gideon the mighty warrior what does he says about the challenge I meet? *"For I know the plans I have for you, declares the Lord, plans to prosper you not to harm you, plans to give you hope and future"*, Jer29:11. This was the letter written to the exiles in Babylon. God saw them tough enough to survive slavery in Babylon and take hold of his promises. In God's mind you are prosperous, you are extremely excellent. That's the character he gives you. Yours is to ask, "Lord what to do now since I'm extremely excellent that will make me shine in the dark?" Even in tough situations you find yourself in, know that there's somebody who think that you are strong enough to turn nothing into something, Somebody who want to give you hope and the desired future. A person who is wise enough to heed what the Lord says to these exiles will go out of his way to find out what exactly are those plans. He will dream the impossible and do the extra-ordinaries just to catch the meaning of those plans. He will understand that troubles are not there to harm him but to get him out of his comfort zone, and that, difficulties are there to remind him that there's something he ought to do that he is not doing.

Without a good character you as good as dead.
A person who doesn't possess a good character is very ignorant. Instead of dreaming his future he complies with every lousy talk coming from the very same people as him. "Who do you think you are to be successful?" this are the words most said by people who hate to see the success of their fellows. They cut your wings while flying and once you fall they laugh. "Forget it my friend it will never happen, this can only be done by wise people not you." They make sure you never get up. Even

when you have told yourself that after each and every stumble you will get up they sweep off the idea from your mind. And yourself; because you don't possess a good character you lie sheepishly where you have fallen asking an irrelevant question, "whom was I to come up with such an idea." The relevant question you should be asking is who I am not to have big dreams?" Everything is possible to those who believe, Mark9:23. This understatement doesn't imply only to good things or success; even failure is possible when you believe in it. God is so willing to grant us according to the way we believe because he doesn't force anything upon us. He gave us the right to choice and he doesn't account for it, regardless of his image we carry.

It is very painful to hear young people, whom we regard as future speaking failure with their mouth, "If so and so didn't achieve what will make me achieve?" with young people like these future is doomed. They are ghosts with flesh and bones on, and it is very scary to live with ghosts. Hence I said without a good character you are as good as dead. Stop comparing yourself with other people for you don't know their challenges in life and how they dealt with them, rather focus on turning your life over.

Good character is built up by confidence. So for you to have a good character you need to be confident about yourself. A husband without confidence is like a sheep in his own house. Kids misbehave, everything falls apart he remains quiet. His wife will talk as bad as she wants with him he will remain tranquil. Even people on the street knows that a father of that house is absent on his present. No matter how bad he can be provoked he won't say enough. Hence women are advised to stroke their husbands' ego because without it they are as good as dead. Each and every husband has an ego that best suit him, so instead of killing it stroke it.

View yourself according to the way God does.
God wanted to make Moses his mouthpiece but Moses picked a serious argument with him. He said, *"I don't know how to speak."* The argument went farther to a point where God's anger burned against him and he appointed Aaron to help him. Even when God said, I will teach you what to say, still Moses refused and said send someone else. Why someone else? Can someone like God err? Even to this day we still have people like Moses; when God says you are going to be successful, they say, "excuse me God! I think you have made a mistake, how can somebody like me be successful? Go and try my neighbor, not me." "God is too wise to err." When God says you are a winner stop counting how many battles you still need to fight or have lost. Don't count how many times you have fallen in battle, let him do the counting. Yours is to say yes Lord whatever you say I am; I am. It is highly impossible for God to lie. When He says you are successful irrespective of the circumstances you are successful, because immediately He says you are the situation will turn in your favor. God needs your yes to perform things, as he needed Moses' and Gidion's.

Too long is the journey of life and many are the obstacles we come across, but it doesn't mean that there's no way forward. When the Israelites where approaching the Red sea the Egyptians were right after them. The Israelites were terrified, but God came with the message of hope. He said; *"the Egyptians that you see today you will never see again."* Ex14:10-13. Every obstacle you meet on the way is to your advantage not to meet in future. So do not be discouraged look forward and trust God. He doesn't look you according to the way the situations or people do. When the situation says, "I've held you tight you are going nowhere."God says keep moving so that you don't deal with the same situation over and over again. The circumstances around us are not defining us, but it all depends on the way you as an individual view yourself. I might wear rags but it doesn't mean I'll always wear them until I die. I might stay in a shack but it doesn't mean there's nothing good that will come out of me. All circumstances around us only mean temporary conditions. Collins concise dictionary define circumstance as an incident or occurrence especially the one by chance. Don't tell me that you define yourself according to an incident! It is by a chance that things are not working well for you. Keep moving it's only for a while. When looking at you; people might see a looser, but God see more than a conquer, an achiever and the person with high intelligence that nothing can stop him from achieving what he put on his mind. How do you view yourself? There is absolutely nothing on earth that can stop you from achieving what you want in life; neither money nor poverty, only if you are willing to utilize your brains. God himself said so. *"The Lord said, if as one people speaking the same language they have begun to do this, then nothing they plan to do will be impossible for them." Gen 11:6*

From verse 3 we see how intelligent these people were. They wanted to built a tower "that reaches heaven so that they never be scattered over the face of the whole earth. This was their dream. *"They said to each other come, let's make bricks and bake them thoroughly. They used brick instead of stones and bitumen for mortar."Vs 3*

The character we notice here is the character of a dreamer. Not just a dreamer, but a dreamer who inherited this character from God the father. Their dream had a direction; they were building a tower that reaches heaven. How is that possible? From above your head how far is heaven? No matter how tall you maybe heaven is out of reach. So imagine people building a tower that reaches heaven, how long will that take?

The dreamer visualizes the end in the beginning. They were not concerned about time as long as their tower reached heaven, as long as they achieved their dream. This doesn't remind you of God when he created the universe? They wanted to make the name for themselves, and also not to be scatted in the face of the earth. Their dream was supported by reasons why they wanted to build that specific tower. From them we learn that a dreamer must have motives why he wants things to happen in a way he chooses. This also remind us of God when he created man, His motives was him to carry his image and rule over everything he created. To prepare for their dream, these men called one another and baked bricks thoroughly. A dreamer when preparing for his dream he ensures that everything is in order to avoid unnecessary disturbance. God before creating man he made sure that the earth was in perfect order. The bible tells us that they used bricks instead of stone and bitumen for mortar; this shows that they wanted their tower to be unique and very special. By unique and special I mean it should be distinguished, without equal and excelling others of its kind. A dreamer moves out of the ordinary to the extra ordinary. Stones were there but not suitable to build this distinguished tower and mortar was not good enough for it as well. When looking at this man God saw himself in them, for this reason God said, *"Nothing will be impossible for them."* It's like God was saying I know myself and these are my images and my likeness, if I have created the universe out of nothing; without any hindrance what will hinder them? The men of Babel didn't look the conditions around them. They didn't look at what they didn't have instead they utilized what they had to create what they lacked. Nothing is out of reach for a man with inspiration who believes that he has got what it takes. Are you a dreamer? Then view yourself according to the way God does so that you make things happen. When God looks at you he sees himself in you, there is nothing that can hinder him and you likewise.

1Samuel 16:1-13 tells a story of a young boy who was never thought to be a king. When his father and his brother were meeting a well known prophet of that time Samuel he wasn't even invited. His father saw a young boy, but God saw a king, when he saw a sheep tender

God saw a leader. *"So he asked Jesse, are all these sons you have? Jesse answered, there is still the youngest, but he is tending sheep. Samuel said, send for him we will not sit down until he arrived." V11*

This scripture illustrate how little people think about others. If they don't see themselves as achievers what makes you think they will see you as one? So many times we heard about Joseph and his dreams but we don't follow what the story teaches. This proves that we love hearing stories but are not wise to keep up with what they teach. Joseph was a young person like you and I. He had an extra-ordinary dream but for the fact that his family was used to ordinary dreams they took him for a fool. His father ridiculed and said, *"What is this dream you had? Will your mother, I and your brothers actually come and bow down to the ground before you."* Gen37:10

Poor Joseph wasn't even aware of how great is the meaning of his dream. Dream in a way that will startle everyone around you, you have the ability to. Once you have started work towards achieving it because it is of no use to have a dream that you won't follow.

Joseph's dream was a threat to his family. It should have been an insult to Jacob; he couldn't imagine himself bowing down before young Joseph. He had a history of wrestling with God, Gen38:28. His history wouldn't allow him to bow before young Joseph. I believe that by saying what dream is this he was simply saying, "No, not you my son, you can't have this kind of dream."

When God says he cans which means he can. After wrestling with God, God said to him, *"You name will no longer be Jacob, but Israel, because you have fought with God and with men and have overcome."* Now, who was Joseph that he should bow down before? He had not won any battle with men, not to mention God yet he claims that Jacob the "wrestler" and the whole family will bow down before him! That's ridiculous! God does the ridiculous things to shame the ones we regard highly, he does the unbelievable. Didn't Joseph reach his dream? Of course he did. Though he met so many challenges he continued until he defeated. His brothers pushed him in a pit and later sold him to the Egyptians, but it did affect his dream. Later in Egypt Pharo's wife conspired against him and he was thrown into prison, but through it all he conquered and it was after that, that his dream became a reality. He didn't sit down and blame his brothers for hating him; he did shine even in prison. If you are good at what you do nothing can stand your way, even jealousy. Whether they speak badly about you or put you in an awkward position where they think you will not be able to perform, for the fact that once good always good, you will still do good. No one will be able to fill your space, and your absence will always be notable.

Don't give up, the circumstance you meet along the journey are not worth the privilege of reaching your dream. Some of the challenges are just there to elevate you to your dream. Joseph's story encourages us to dream and share our dreams with people around us so that they criticize, and once they criticize we get a forward push. You never know, maybe some are criticizing because they are jealous. *"His brothers were jealous of him", Gen37:11.* And some are like Joseph's father, they ridicule just to distract but keep the matter in mind. The former characters understood Joseph's dream better than him and they wanted to destroy it while he was still pregnant with it so that he gives birth to air. We always have the former characters in our lives. Sometimes these characters are the most trusted once, but never abort your dream because of them. Their jealousy would not let you be better than them. Never hate them, you need them, without them your life will be quiet and boring. Like a spring allow them to hard press you; once they release jump to where they will never see you again. Sometimes use them as your motive to dream, not necessarily that they are but just to keep yourself focused. Knowing that there's someone who is watching and waiting for you to err will keep you focused. Once you overcome they are the ones who will give testimonies about you and sing your praises.

When God created man in his image and likeness, he actually wanted him to inherit his character of seeing the end in the beginning and the future in the present time. For instance man was not yet formed but God saw him as a ruler of the earth. Your dreams are not yet, but see yourself successful in them.

YOUR IDENTITY IS INFLUENCED BY YOUR CHARACTER; YOUR CHARATER IS WHAT GOD THINKS OF YOU.

Chapter 2

Your success is buried within you.

"But when he asks, he must believe and not doubt, because he who doubts is like the wave of the sea, blowing and tossed by the wind, Jam1:6.

Have you ever seen the wave of the sea, every where the wind point it goes, so is the person without faith. Wherever people points he goes without any hesitation. For instance if I can say to him you are an artist, he will quickly start singing, but let someone enter right on the spot and point to the opposite direction, he will leave the mikes and the key boards to the other direction. In the beginning the earth was formless but God was not formless, that is why he took one step at time until everything was thoroughly. At the beginning of your road to success things might seem so complicated and you might not be sure whether things will work out, but focus and have faith.

Faith works only with two rules.
Rule number one: I am possible, that's what faith tells you.
Rule number two: When things are not possible go back to rule number one.
This means there is nothing under the sun which is impossible, because faith makes everything possible. Look at where we apply faith, we don't apply faith to the difficulties, but we apply faith to the impossible.

Wherever in your life you meet the impossible just substitute the word impossible with rule number one of faith I'm possible. If you have applied rule number one and things seem not to change move to rule number two. It sounds easy doesn't it?

Faith it is a fixed point that whatever believed will surely come to pass. It is not affected by the surrounding, and not influenced by the impossible, in fact it affect the surrounding and influence the impossible. I might not be the good singer in the beginning but with faith I'll end up being the good one, and I won't give up until I become one. That's how the person with faith speaks.

Faith is a strong or unshakeable belief in something especial without a proof. When it says unshakeable which means there are things trying to shake it but it remains firm. A person with faith is unshakeable, no matter how many obstacles he meets along the journey or how many people gives up on the journey, he keeps moving as though he has got what he longed for. He doesn't focus to what hinders others but to the great achievement he will get once he overcomes. He doesn't allow insecurities to move him on his path.

Faith is supported by hope and without hope faith is dead. When the bible speaks about hope it says, *"We have this hope as an anchor for the soul, firm and secure."* *Heb 6:19*

Let us try to perceive and anchor, what is an anchor? An anchor is a device attached to a vessel by cable and dropped overboard so as to grip the bottom and restrict movement, or it can be explained as an object that is used to hold something else firmly in place. When for instance the wind arouses with the ship in the sea, an anchor will be thrown in water in order to restrict the movement of the ship. The ship will depend on an anchor to control its movement. It will forget about how strong is the wind and how far it is from the destination but it will trust on the anchor to hold it firmly until it reach its destination. Be like this ship which is not threatened by the wind or the distance, keep hoping that you will make it through. Let people talk all they want, let them criticize to their last breath, but let your hope restrict your movement and hold you firmly to one direction so that you never detour. Your hope will prevent you from being like Saul who failed on the lasts minutes. *"What have you done? Samuel asked. Saul replied, when I saw that the men were scattering, and that you did not come at the set time and the philistine were assembling at Michmash, I thought now the philistines will come against me at Gilgal and I have not sought the face of the Lord" 1Sam13:11-12.*

In 1Sam10:8 the bible tells us that Samuel sent Saul ahead of him to Gilgal assuring that he will surely come to him to sacrifice a burned offering and a fellowship offering but he must wait for seven days until he comes. At Gilgal Saul met with challenges and he couldn't deal with them. He dropped off his hope and unfortunately that act caused his family the kingship. God was going to establish the kingdom of Israel through his family. The first challenge he met is: Samuel didn't come right at the set time. Secondly the troops with him were quaking with fear and he himself was afraid. And thirdly some of the men were scattering from him. Keep these challenges in mind we will discuss them latter. Under this circumstances Saul was compelled to act. He did act but he acted foolishly. He sent for the offerings and offered them himself; right after he had presented them Samuel arrived. At the beginning of the seven days he hoped that Samuel will come but when that period passed he allowed fear to take over. He failed in the last minutes. Instead of celebrating he was now ashamed of himself.

Let's take Saul's story to today's life and try to elaborate his challenges in a conspicuous way. You find a beautiful young lady behaving so well and abstaining from sex waiting for the man who will say you are the rib of my ribs. But to her misfortune when she turns and look around everyone is getting married, everyone has a child and she is the only one who is left behind. These are the three challenges that Saul met. No one wants to be left behind; everyone wants to keep up with the standard of life. Under these circumstances the poor lady will start being worried; soon fear will take over and compel her to find herself a man to date. And this because will be done under pressure she will throw herself to any man who promise love. Right after she had thrown her hope away, there comes MR right saying, "I've been watching you all along, and now I am ready to make you mine and travel the world with you." By that time those words will mean nothing to her because she would have already committed herself to a man whom God didn't bless her with, and because he is not from God her marriage will be a very miserable one. All these years she waited in vain. Instead of receiving the grown of glory she receives an insult. Please! Don't throw your hope away for it will reward you. When your dream is delayed it doesn't mean that it is denied.

In some cases you find a guy dating a lady whom she loves most, but due to unemployment he can't satisfy her financially. In the beginning of the relationship the lady will comfort and support the guy in every way she can. You know them; they are very good at playing towers of strength. But once she realizes that she has been waiting for a long time and things are not getting any better. She will start complaining about everything the man does, and once she complains it means she can't take it any longer. Hope has disappeared bit by bit; from there she will find herself a man who can satisfy her. Only to find out when she is pregnant that the minister of finance she is dating is a married man and he will never leave his family for her. Bad things happen when we become hopeless. Rom 5:5 says hope doesn't disappoint us. Keep hoping no matter the situation you will never be disappointed.

Stop working haphazardly, focus.
The work of a person without focus is fruitless. Whenever he starts working when something appears that seems to be better than what he does he leave his work unfinished and move to next. Finish the former then move to the rest. He doesn't have a steady goal for he works for the sake of working, plan for the sake of planning and dream for the sake of dreaming. Nothing is serious about him. He doesn't even have reasons for

doing whatsoever he does. His reasons are composed about lots of maybes. "Maybe I will achieve this one, maybe it will get me to the next level." Maybe, maybe.......... when you can introduce drums he will compose a kwaito song, because you don't need many words to compose a kwaito song. Give your dream time to develop and grow, once it has; direct it in a path where it will be able to mature, then you will harvest the desired fruits. Stop taking things for granted, when God started the universe he started with the words let there be light. With light the universe was far from being complete and not yet begun, however God managed to focus until the earth was established. Light represent hope. I want you to take a solitude time, do an introspection and be patient with yourself. What is it that thing which you have, which can serve as light/hope? No matter how small it is pursue it until you see the whole part of it.

When Elisha met the widow whom her children were about to be taken as slaves to pay for her husband's credits, Elisha asked, *"What do you have in your house." Elisha replied to her, how can I help you? Tell me what do you have in your house?"* The woman's help was not in Elisha but right in her house. Same applies to you the answer that you need it is right in your mind, search for it. When Elisha asked, "How can I help you?" he was simply saying, "Woman give me direction then I will help you". That is the same question that God asks when receiving your request. Those who get their answers are the ones who give him a specific direction. Those who work haphazardly they will always find it difficult to point where they actually need help because they've got plenty places to point. They will start singing their song again, "maybe this one will do, or maybe this one it's much quicker." Have a focal point; stop confusing yourself because God is of order not confusion. Here is a trick question to those who don't focus in one thing at a time, "Tell me what you have in your house?" Now; this question makes it clear that the woman's help was right in her house; she just needed God to bless it so that it can be of use to her. Sometimes we do have things that can help us, but if they are not blessed by God they are equals to nothing. Psalm127 says, *"if the Lord doesn't build the house the builders build in vain."* So whatever you do if God does not approve it; it's in vain.

Your breakthrough is right in your mind, you don't need a Sangoma to throw bones and say,"The ancestors have spoken; they say you must fetch your help from the river."
No! Your help is within you it's just that God hasn't approved it because you have not prayed about it. Your mind is like a kitchen where menus are being prepared. When God "the chef" asks for a menu you must give him a well prepared menu, and he will do the cooking. Some people are in habit of impressing God with things that are not impressing. When He asks, "What do you have in mind?" They say, "Plenty of ideas". How is that person going to get help from God if he doesn't know where he needs help? A person like that is the same as the one who says that there are no jobs but has not posted a single curriculum vitae. I mean how will he get a job if he won't apply? When you ask from God be

specific, tell God that you want to open a huge salon and you need his guidance, that's all. Don't say if the salon doesn't work I would go for acting. With God it doesn't work like that. You pray for something and wait until you receive. I like this widow, when Elisha asked what you have in your house, she pointed straight to a thing which she thought could be of help. "Your servant has nothing there at all, she said except the little oil". I believe that there were many more households, but at that pointing time there were of no use to the woman except the little oil. I want you to give a thought to this one, how can the little oil pay for the debts that the widow's husbands failed to pay while he was alive? It should have cost this widow faith to believe that with that little oil the man of God can perform a miracle. The person who has focus is like this woman his arrow shoot straight to the target. He comes to God with a complete idea. I use the term idea because there's somewhere I want us to get. An idea is the vague belief that lead to greater things if followed, there we are. The little oil produced a good deal of oil. So that vague idea that you have right now will give birth to greater things if you follow it closely.

On the first day God created light not lights. I don't know how clear that light was but I know that God began his work with it. Note! There were neither stars nor the sun but God managed to work on it until he was sure enough that he needed to add on that light.

In the beginning of your path the road might seem so dark that you wish you had never begun, but bear in mind that you will only make it through when you focus. Sometimes it might seem like you don't have what it takes, but for the mare fact that you've got the idea refuse to give up. You are God's image; you have the ability of generating your light out of nowhere. Whenever you see the small ray of light know that there is a big portion of it on the other end waiting for you. We are never given dreams without been given the power to reach them. Stop being a jack of all trades whom his goal is to master none.

Be the prophet of your own life.
"The tongue has the power of life and death and those who love it will eat its fruit. Prov18:21
This is one of the verses that proves without any reasonable doubt that you success is within you. When you speak failure with your mouth; the very same failure comes from within you and becomes you. Here the bible teaches us to restrict our tongues because they've got the power to destroy or build us. Speak good things about yourself. This will grow your dream big because you know you have what it takes. We are what we think and speak with our mouth. Respect is not demanded but earned. Normally people listen to what you say and watch how you behave before they can respect you. Who will want to respect a person who thinks that he is worth nothing? Even being in the company of a person who thinks like that is waste of time because you won't benefit anything from him; he will feed your mind with nonsense. What you think is what you say and what you say becomes your life style. For instance, if you say you are a looser you will gradually act like one until you become one. There is this thing that I don't like about

people, when they've got no money they call themselves dogs. You hear a person saying I've got nothing I am a dog. Let me tell you if you say you are a dog, you are. Instead of talking you will bark like one (a person who speaks a senseless thing barks). Instead of working you will lie around and instead of planning you will sleep. Remember we are unique and special, so when you call yourself a dog you mean that you are a distinguished dog without its equal and excelling others of its kind. Is it a right way to describe yourself? You can do better than that. The disadvantage of describing yourself in that manner is that people will also treat you like a dog because people do to you what you allow them to. Prov13:3 says, *"He who guards his tongue guards his life, but he who speaks rashly will come to ruin."* Stop ruining your life with useless words. Prophesy only what is good for your life. Speak only what is building your character or else keep your mouth shut and pray unto God to help you. You are God's masterpiece; any bad label doesn't suit you. Start saying good things about yourself now.

Fear is the weapon of the devil.

The devil uses fear to hinder us from realizing that we are unbeatable. Fear is the opposite of faith. If you are controlled by it; know that you are carrying the weapon of the devil within yourself. The thing that people fear the most is to take the first step, they should fear the opposite instead. This is the common question they tend to ask themselves. What if I fail? And they forget to ask that what if I don't fail. Fear is what kills us most and what keeps us in poverty. We fear to begin our own projects so that we benefit ourselves and other people. What if we don't succeed it is simple to answer. If we don't succeed we go back to the main plan and see where the mistake has occurred. A sage has once said, *"Turn failure into fertilizers and make it grow."* So when you fail it shouldn't worry you because you are gathering fertilizers for your success. The person who hadn't taken the first step has no fertilizers for his success. Don't be afraid of the word failure and its meaning because if you can focus on that you will lose the greater advantage of it. Failure molds your character and makes you courteous. It builds a stronger person out of you and removes all the fear.

What will people say? This is a question that we tend to ask again when we allowed fear. Even the answer of this one is simple. What are they saying when you are sitting and doing nothing? The very same thing they are saying when you are doing nothing is what they will say when you start doing something. So never mind them; their saying is not worth your success. When a car is not moving, the dogs take shelter under its shadow, but once the car moves the very same dogs' barks at it. No matter how loud the dogs bark at the car; it will never stop moving because of them. What I'm saying is that, the dog barks at the moving car so as people. When they talk about you it simply shows that you are living and doing something that they are not doing. *Isaiah 50:6 says, "I offered my back to those who beat, my cheeks to those who pulled out my beard; I did not hide my face to those who spit."* Do likewise. Don't fear those who criticize you. Infect give them your back to beat as hard as they want. While beating they push you forward. They are the ones who will make your success possible. Those who mock will be the one' singing your praises in future.

Push your way through.
Once you have overcome your fears push your way through. Be determined for there's nothing that could get in the way of a determined person.

Is27:3-4, *"Sing about the fruitful vineyard: I the Lord watch over it, I water it continually. I guard it day and night, so that no-one may harm it."* Here we learn about the vineyard which the Lord loves. He nourishes it continually and to ensure that no one harms it; he guards it day and night. Do the same with your dream. Enrich it with things that will make it come true. God continues by saying only if there were barriers confronting me, I would match against them in battle, I will set them on fire. Again, do the same with your dream. If there are things confronting you match against them, set them on fire, do whatever it take to remove them. Frankly, I advise you to avoid doing nothing because you will end up being a looser.

Turn a disadvantage into an advantage.
Zacharias because of his shortness was able to see Jesus in a very close rage than most people. How? Because he didn't sit down and complain to taller people that they are hindering him from seeing Jesus; instead he ran to the tree which he thought Jesus will pass nearby and climbed it. His act invited Jesus attention and latter he

joined Him in his own house. From Zacharias we learn that we can easily turn our disadvantage into an advantage. I didn't have money to go to varsity to further my studies, that is my disadvantage, but had I have gone to university I wouldn't have written this book, because I would have been so preoccupied with my studies without realizing the potential in me. You see, it has worked for me. There are no bad things in life it is just the matter of how we choose to respond to a given situation. Now start searching how you can turn you disadvantage into an advantage. Even if you can go to the people who are very successful in life and listen to their testimonies you will find that it is their disadvantage that put them where they are today. If they did it what will stop you from doing the same?

Ecc9:11 says, *"I have seen this under the sun: the race is not to swift or the battle to the strong, nor does food come to the wise; but chance happen to them all."* How many times chances come your way and you push them over? You hear people saying if I had another chance in life but once that chance comes they push it over. Most of the people who are struggling today are the ones who have pushed away opportunities thinking that something better will come. Sometimes success comes wearing a dirty overall; you need to clean it and make it look the way you will want it. It was not easy for me to pen down this book, but for the fact that I knew that where there's will there's a way I did and you are reading it now. From the scripture coded we learn to recognize our seasons and times in life. Bear in mind; even when it is your time and season it doesn't mean things will come easy without you working hard for them.

PLEASE KEEP THESE IN MIND!!!
Your success is right in your mind, failure isn't bad as you think, your disadvantage can be your advantage, notice your season and time and Stop passing over opportunities regularly.

Chapter 3

Mistake is the best teacher.

"Then Shechaniah son of Jehiel, one of the decadents of Elam; said to Ezra; we have been unfaithful against our God by intermarrying foreign women from the people around us. But in spite of this, there is still hope for Israel."
Ezra10:2

The Israelites made a mistake of inter marrying with foreigners or other nations whom God warned them not to. They did what God forbidden. These nations had their gods and practices which Israel had to separate itself from because they served the Holy God. However Israel failed to follow the instruction. When we talk about Israel we talk about the nation that knew God bests than any other nations. They knew him through his miracles and terrors. They suffered his punishment and discipline. They saw him fighting their battles and most of them all they have experienced his love and jealousy. They knew that when God says NO, it is a big resounding NO without any but. God wanted Israel to remain holly and sacred for him, hence he wouldn't allow it to sully itself unnecessarily. But we see Israel behaving like a dove, easily deceived and senseless. Though God has warned them to be not enticed by other nations they stood against that warning. They abandoned their God whom had led them to where they

are for new gods whom they just knew. These shows how easily people forget, a minute is more than enough to forget all the good you have done for them.
What I like about the Israelites is that; when they realized that they've made a mistake they took immediate steps to correct it. They gathered around Ezra and wept before the Lord. This was to say: "God we are aware of our mistake please forgive us." Imagine if it were you; how would you have dealt with the situation? I'm sure you would have said what's done is done and continued living with the mistake. Sometimes we as people can be very ignorant. The Israelites in adding to their repentance they sent away their foreign wives and children. Once you have admitted that you have made a mistake which steps do you take to correct it?

We are living in the obnoxious world, where people remain obstreperous. In circumstances like this everything remain obscure. It is very difficult to separate between right and wrong, and between truth and lies. You find people applauding and encouraging a very wrong act but scoffing and criticizing a very good one. The arbiters permit acts which are contrary to the word of God and which perverts human's conducts just to please the majority. I'd rather stand alone and do the right thing than following a group of people doing the opposite. If the majority does the wrong thing; to me that means all fools are on the same side and there's no one to guide because they are all alike. Some people find it difficult to believe that there is God and he has created man and everything in the world yet they believe that man has evolved from a monkey. Psalm14:1 say *a fool has said in his heart there is no God.* Somebody has ever wrote that the person who says there is no God is like a mouse eating bread in the dark, with its mouth full of bread it confesses, "I don't believe there's such a thing called the baker." People who commit murder are thrown into jail but those who do abortion are patted on the shoulder for the job well done. To me there's no difference between the two. I was just trying to illustrate the world we are living in.

We are living in an obstreperous world where everyone remains obstinate. In a world like this mistakes collides time and again, yet one must bear in mind that a mistake that is never corrected in time will create a vicious circle and make one more oblivious to danger. With our eyes wide open we find ourselves lost, falling and without the knowledge of what to do next. Those who are wise enough allows a mistake to teach them not to block their way forward. They don't allow a mistake to obliterate their courage, but they continue believing that there is still hope. After a fall they get up; shook off the dust and start moving again. After abjection they accrue every piece of their lives and start building again. They first admit that they've made a mistake and get their life back on track while correcting the mistake. They take the lesson that the mistake have brought about and stay a mile away from something that could lead to it again. A fool is the one who doesn't learn anything from his mistakes but repeat one thing again and again. Such a person is not willing to grow.

Get up after a fall.

We've got a problem of people who would not get up after a fall. They just lie where they have fallen and tell everyone who seem to pity them that they have fallen. There's nothing attractive about lying were you have fallen but there is something inspiring about getting up after a stumble. You become a hero or a heroin because true heroes and heroines lies within each one of us, but once you lie where you have fallen you remain a zero. Many teenagers quit school after failing a grade. It doesn't mean when they quit school they will go to another grade, in fact they will remain there for the rest of their lives. There's nothing wrong about failing. Every time you fail you need to check your mistakes and start again with more effort until you get it right. So many times people fail and feel ashamed of getting up, the question I ask myself is that why can't they feel ashamed of the opposite. That fall was never meant to keep you down but to keep you alert. When you fall don't drop down your hope but keep it with you so that it raises you. No matter how far you have fallen from the top, your hope will help you to get there again. Haven't you heard that the most fallen can rise up again? The only glue that holds people down after a fall is being hopeless, besides it there's no other. So remove that glue from your mind.

The people who surprise me are the ones who fall up, those who don't know how they got to the top but they just found themselves on top. There is a big difference between the person who fall from up and the one who fall up. Those who fall from up they easily get their way up again, but those who fall up (who finds themselves up) once they fall they find it difficult to get to the top again. I'm talking about those who bribed their way to the top, inherited business from their late fathers. I'm not implying that it is bad to inherit a business, all I'm saying is that; learn everything about the business, because if you don't; when you fall you won't even get a glimpse of building it all over again. Be happy when you fall from up to down rather than from down to up.

Admit your mistake.
From the scripture read we hear Shechaniah giving a brief repentant statement, *"We have been unfaithful to God."* He took the blame to himself and others. He didn't blame it on the beauty of those foreign women or the manner they displayed towards them. This is the challenge that we face most of the time. When a person has done something wrong, he wouldn't swallow his pride and say sorry it was the mistake and it would never happen again. A person would rather hurt his fellow rather than admitting his mistake. Many marriages have hit the rock because everyone is so perfect to admit when he is wrong or if he does admit he comes up with excuses to cover up his action. When I'm saying "he" I'm not referring to males only but I'm addressing everyone. Excuses can only cover you for a while but once the cover is blown you will be left in public with nowhere to hide. So many times I heard husbands cheat on their wives and when asked they say it is their nature. They were created like that. They say all men are cheaters. I wonder where that comes from. We as human beings got this tendency of justifying every wrong we do. God didn't create an adulterer but a pure man. Out off the ribs of that created man he

removed one rib and created a woman with it. *"Then Lord God made a woman from the rib he had taken out of the man and he brought her to the man."* Gen2:22
This was after God saw that Adam needed a helper not helpers. Unfortunately whether men like it or not that is how marriage was created by God. When God created Eve he didn't create just a helper but *"a suitable helper"* for her husband. This proves without any reasonable doubt that every woman is suitable for her husband. Irrespective of the changes she undergoes after marriage. Whether she grows fat or become thin, or whether she complains a lot; for the fact that God said she is suitable for you then she is, you don't have any right to go out and look for those whom you think they might be good for you.

A person who refuses to acknowledge his mistake is like the one who dig a huge pit on his way and leaves it uncovered, later when passing there, unmindful, he falls into it and break his foot. He will continue breaking himself on that pit until he decides to close it. If he doesn't close it he will even die from it. When you acknowledge your mistake and never repeat it again it shows that you have grown and have learned something. The problem with us is that we are very lazy to learn; even learning from our own experiences becomes difficult. I don't know why because you don't pay any penny when learning from your mistakes. A mistake that is never admitted keeps you where you are. If you should have been a matured husband it keeps you at stage of being an immature play boy. Admit your mistake, and don't be like the one who eat and wipes his mouth and say "I haven't done anything wrong." Many marriages are noisy; we are even scared of getting married because of such marriages, they portray too much of violence and advertise too much of divorce. I repeat it again admit your mistake; stop decorating it with lies.

Stop blaming other people for your own mistake.

The only person who has the power to control your life is you. Even the omniscient God doesn't control us, because he created us to be human beings with the ability to choose not to be robots that he can control. I can be your wife, friend or mentor but it doesn't mean I can decide for you. The only part that I can play is to advice you but the final decision is left with you. Even when I have offered you my advice it doesn't mean when it back fires I am accountable. Remember I only offered an advice I didn't enter your brain and decide for you. So when it back fires you have no right to blame me because you could have decided against it. The only life I am accountable for is mine and I can't afford the extra work of being responsible for another adult like me. When making any decision be sure it is what you want; irrespective of whom the advice comes from.

Let's go a little back in Genesis to our friend Adam. He ate from the tree he wasn't supposed to. When God asked why had he done that he shifted the blame to Eve as if Eve threaten to kill him if doesn't eat of the tree. He also blamed God as if God planned his down fall by bringing forth Eve. He said, *"The woman you put here with me- she gave me some of the fruits from the tree and I ate." Gen3:17*

That's our nature as human beings; we are never wrong and irrelevant when answering. God's question was, "have you eaten from the tree I commanded you not to eat?" The question needed a simple yes or no. He should have said yes God I did and am sorry for not obeying. God came to Eve whom was unreliable like her husband and she also pushed the blame forward. The Lord God said to the woman, "what is this you have done?" In simple God was simply saying woman confess your sin; not somebody's sin but yours, tell me where you have gone wrong. Eve was also too perfect to take the blame she blamed the snake forgetting that the commandment was not given to the snake but to Adam who later passed it to her. I wonder how would the serpent answered had God asked it.

Some people have died, some are in prison and other in hospitals because of this understatement "It was never my mistake." It is painful because some had gone down to grave not forgiven by God and people. Because it was never their mistake they took no means to correct it; it devoured them until they were finished. Though they argued to confess; their conscious knew the truth and it wouldn't let them live in peace. Those who are in prison and hospitals will come back to their unchanged lives because it was never their mistake that were locked in prison or laid in the hospital. Only if they will admit that my life has turned out like this because I only chose to listen to bad advices it would be easier for them to correct their ways. Stop pointing a finger to your friends but point it back to you. Take it into consideration that when you point a finger to another person three point back to you; meaning you are three times responsible. If they are responsible for misleading your life you are three times responsible than them.

This manner of pointing a finger on one another it is worse in marriages. It is always, "I did it because you have done this and that." This is not good and must not happen. You find one mistake repeated several times in different ways because the couples are in a competition of who can make the worse mistake than the other. Pastors, friends and counselors tried to keep such marriages from falling apart but it became formidable. No one wants to back down.

Mistakes are not bad as they sound in fact they have wrapped a great lesson that is vital for life within them, and your success need that lesson.

Admit your mistake, confess it and never repeat it again. Take the lesson it has brought about.

Admit your mistake. Part2

"I cried to him with my mouth, his praise was on my tongue. If I had cherished sin in my heart, the Lord would have not listened. But God has surely listened and heard my voice in prayer" Psalm66:17-18.

People need help but they refuse to tell the cause of their problem. Every cause has the effect and likewise every choice has the consequences. They are afraid of being on the wrong, they want people think that they never mistake. Here the psalmist gives us an example of a person who has admitted and confessed his mistake.

Because of the step that he took God had no reason to refuse listening to him. He says "in the mist of my problems I cried to God. I didn't hide anything from him. I purified my heart by taking out all the sin that made its dwell within me. I renounce my pride and when looking at me God saw nothing that hinders him from helping me. In no way you can help a person who doesn't admit his mistake. Trust me when saying you are likely to deal with the wrong problem because you are dealing with the wrong person. When the person says it is so and so who did this, it means you must leave him and go to so and so. Take an example of a child who steal sugar and says it is not me and point the other kid who didn't even dare touch it.

When you can take a look to the problems we meet, you will find out that fifty percent of them are caused by the mistakes that we do and never care to correct. When one mistake is repeated over and over we no longer call it a mistake but a problem. That's why you hear most of the time people saying "he has got a drinking problem", it started as a mistake until it became a problem. My advice to you: admit your mistake and deal with it before it becomes a problem.

A mistake it's dangerous when its purpose it's never fulfilled.

A mistake is a Messenger that is sent to give a special lesson. It gives you a chance to do an introspection with questions like, where have I gone wrong, how did I get these consequences and what should be done to avoid them next time. It enables you to find a stronger sense of who you are and you become a much organized person, the masterpiece that God created you to be. A mistake is a corrector and a reminder. It corrects your attitude and sometimes leaves scars that will remind you not to play on fire again.

Now, if this purposes are not attained the person will remain stiff-neck and without wisdom and knowledge. He will remain estranged to God and become a problem to other people. He will grow more stupid than ever, even when he got burned the first time he will put his hand back on fire again thinking that he will not burn this time. Take an example of girls who are promised marriage and left pregnant. Some of them don't say the first one has disappointed me, let me focus on raising this child and leave boys alone, rather, they move to next who will probably do the same and the next and the next until they have four children with different fathers. In her mind she thinks this one has money maybe he will marry me. This one seems to be matured than the first two so he has to marry me, only to find out that he is also a passerby. When are you going to learn? Isn't that being stiff neck? Be wise, you have been hurt the first time, run a mile away from sex before marriage. Let those scars of being told right in the eyes that this pregnancy is not for me be a reminder that sex before marriage is not good. Keep the lesson and it will make you wiser than ever. I'm not saying you should never love, all I'm saying is love with your heart not with your special garden. The person who wants to marry you will marry you even before tasting your garden, if he truly loves you. The bible says, "Stolen water is sweet; food eaten in secret is delicious! But little do they know is that the dead are there."

Here the bible speaks about the woman folly that is undisciplined and without knowledge. The bible says she calls out to those who pass by with those coded words. My message to you is, "do not enjoy stolen water or food eaten in secret because there is death in them and once death is working through you, you come to search help were there's light." Sometimes you will be stealing water with a married man without knowing; only to find out when you are pregnant that you are dating a father of four. You are the one who will feel pain of being humiliated. That thing you once enjoyed will become the one you dread most.

After a stumble get up and allow the mistake to fulfill its purpose. Don't be lazy to learn for you will die before your time. Allow yourself to develop into a better independent individual through your mistakes. How many times must you cry before you can learn? Those who are wise will answer by saying once beaten twice shy, but fools will say as long as I have tears. When a mistake is repeated severally it's no longer a mistake but folly. So don't be a fool because God didn't create fools but individuals with the ability to learn and that possess the high intelligence.

Chapter 4

Pain is change.

"In the year that king Uzziah died, I saw the Lord seated on his throne, high and exalted, and the train of his robe filled the temple", Is6:1.

Uzziah was sixteen years when he started ruling in Israel and he reigned in Jerusalem for fifty-two years. In the beginning of his reign he did what was right in the eyes of the Lord God. With the help of the Lord he defeated many nations and his fame spread because he had become very powerful. But after Uzziah was powerful he became so proud and his pride led to his downfall. He became unfaithful to the Lord and he wouldn't let the priest burn incenses for him. In other words he prevented the priests to perform their duty. These events prevented Isaiah to receive his call of being a prophet from the Lord. Uzziah was the wall between Isaiah and God that needed to be removed. For the fact that he was unfaithful his removal was the permanent one, hence he died. His death must have brought pain to the nation as a whole because he was their king. The agony of death takes long time before it can be removed from people's minds and hearts. Most especial when the death involves the loved one who has worked for the nation, but through it all Isaiah saw the Lord; in the very same year that king Uzziah died. For some people it might take more than a year to mourn for their loved one. While they mourn everything seem to be not so important, their life stuck and they would not open the eyes to see that the world is happening and if they are not present, tough luck it will continue without their presence. It becomes hard for them to move on without the deceased; everything seems impossible. During this event people develop the attitude of questioning God strange questions. Why him Lord? If not him who else, who will agree to die for him? So far it is Jesus only who died for the world. We are not here to stay we have come to leave a mark and go back to our creator.

The scripture read shows us that when there's a door that closes, there is definitely the other one that opens. Only people with open eyes while mourning can manage to see the opening door and walk through it. In simple when God takes something from us he wants to give us something better. If we are still holding on to the old one we would not be able to receive the one which he is about to give because our hands would be full. Though the death of Uzziah was painful but it served as an eye opener to Isaiah. He realized that the Lord needed a person who can be his mouthpiece to the house of Israel. Take this example, when kids still have parents some refuse to grow because they know that their parents will take care of everything. But once the parents die the kids without being told they know that they must stand and do things for themselves. Those who where lazy to work they will start marketing. Had their parents lived they would have remained childish, but now that they are gone they start moving out of their comfort zones.

Uzziah was dead and it was time for Isaiah to get out of his comfort zone and convey the message of the Lord. So many times in our lives after we have felt pain we realize that it was the wake up call. Though the call frightens, but we need to respond to it because it is in our favor and it gives us a strong testimony. Some will tell you that after I was abandoned by the most trusted ones I learned to rely on God and trust him alone. When the most trusted were there; there was no need for him to acknowledge the Lord because he had all the support that he needed. Some will testify that after I was arrested for something I didn't do I learned to choose a good friend from bad ones. Pain always brings us back when we are lost. Pain it's a "wake up call", but to my surprise there are still people who refuse to wake up after receiving this wake up call. They remain there nursing the wound forever without realizing that now it's time to move on. It is not bad to nurse the wound, but ensure that it doesn't consume much of your time. Nurse and walk away because something might come and add on the wound. Realize the lesson the pain has brought about and do what ought to be done, bear in mind that before we organize we must agonize. I'm sure now you get the importance of pain; it helps one to organize. I like Ecc3 when it says there is time for everything; there is time to agonize and there is time to organize. Psalm119:71 give this testimony: *"it was good for me to be afflicted so that I might learn your decrees."* Agree with me when I say pain it isn't all bad it helps one to organize his ways and improves one's dexterity. It is good for developing one into a stronger person, hence those who are wise says what doesn't kill me makes me strong. If the psalmist had not been afflicted he would have remained vile to God. After he was afflicted his eyes were open and he realized that his ways are contrary to the Lord's law. If pain doesn't kill you know that its purpose was to bring the best out on you. V 67 reads, before I was afflicted I went astray, but now I obey your word." Pain doesn't only open our eyes but it also brings back those who went astray. When all is going well some people when lost don't see the necessity of coming back. Let me tell you this, there is a big problem when everything goes well with us, we forget everything (where we come from, whom we are, which purpose do we serve), including God. We become worse than the atheists because with them it is quite clear that they don't believe in God. Joy becomes our God, but wait for the time when the very same joy is snatched away from us. We quickly run to pastors to lay hands upon us. Pain makes us realize that without God we can't do.

The bible in the book of Luke15:11 tell us a parable of the son who went to his father and demanded his share of estate. The bible says not long after that he got together all he had, set for a distant land and there he squandered his wealth in a wild living. While he had money he didn't remember his family that he left behind. He ravishingly ate his money without thinking that tomorrow is coming. For the fact that no one has the ability to predict what life would be tomorrow, famine striked the land he was living in. Now that he has squandered all his wealth in a wild living he began to be in need. When he had money he didn't consider looking for a job but now because all was finished he hired himself to the citizen of that country who sent him to his field to feed pigs. Due to famine he longed to fill his stomach with the pods that the pigs were eating, but no one gave him anything. This situation brought him back to his senses. He remembered that his father's servants had food to spare while "he" the master's son is dying of hunger. He made a decision that he will not die of the situation. Others may but not him. He realized that he had over stayed his welcome on that place and it was time to go home. He was not ashamed of those who saw him leaving to a distant country. He faced the challenge of being humiliated. He is the one the psalmist talks about when saying, "Before I was afflicted I went astray", famine afflicted and brought him back to his home.

This story is not just a parable that Jesus made back then, to this day we still have people like this prodigal son. People who left their homes long ago and they are caught by the nice times. They won't come home before they are afflicted. Some even when they are afflicted will be too ashamed to face people back at home. A prodigal son is better because he didn't leave kids behind, some as I'm writing they have left six children with their aging parents. When the parents die children will be left in danger with no one to take care of them. They will be left to be victims of everyone who come across them. Their abusers will respond by saying, "we are not guilty for their parents neglected them." Children grow up with hatred that cannot be measured, they also turn out to be abusers because they don't know how to love and what is love. All they have ever felt is the coldness of hate.

It is good to be afflicted, but not good to remain in afflictions.

"Now there were four men with leprosy at the entrance of the city gate. They said to each other, "why stay here until we die? If we say we'll go to the city-the famine is there and we will die. And if we stay here, we will die. So let's go over to the camp of the armaments and surrender to them. If they kill us we will die, and if they spare us will live." 2king7:3-4.

Let's go back a little; I said pain is good because it opens our eyes, it brings back those who are lost, and it gives us a lesson; however it's not a place to dwell in. You need to pass through it not rest on it, for it is a place of weeping and no one enjoys weeping. Ecc3:4 say there is time to weep and a time to laugh, a time to mourn and a time to dance. Here Ecclesiastes was simply saying pass through all for there's not much time to waste in one stop. I like the manner in which it is written, it starts with the bad and end with the good. After each and every weep there is laughter and after mourning there is dancing. Hence psalm30:5 *say weeping may remain for a night but rejoicing comes in the morning.* Pain means the era of night, when the night passes we know that it is morning. Pass through the night and walk in the morning. Never delay any long for time wait for no-man. I'm writing this to encourage those who have been caring pain for many years. They need to move out of the shadows of the past, for there is nothing there only the shadows. What happened has happened you need to forgive and forget.

Move.. there's nothing

better you will get even if you decide to hold on to that pain.
Living with pain is the same as living in the dark. People who are living in the dark where there is no light their lives are on danger because tags take advantage of the situation. Same applies to the person who never let go of pain. He is the target of death, at any time he can decide to commit suicide because pain suffers the heart until the heart cannot take it any longer. In the dark people are robbed, so as pain. It steals people's joy and overwhelms them with tears. Even in laughter once a person remember of the pain his heart ache and the joy end in grief. Even when he is not ill his face looks as though he is ill. Pain it's not a permanent stay but those who choose to dwell in it; it devours them until they are finished. Be like these men with leprosy who told themselves that they would not die of their pain. Ask yourself this question, if the bible says weeping may last for a night why am I still carrying this pain even when morning has come? These men with leprosy the scripture is quiet about how long they have stayed in the city gate, but it tells that they did not want to die there; they didn't want to die abandoned. It doesn't matter how long you have been wounded but you don't need to die from that wound.

When reading Jeremiah10:19; we hear these words, *"woe to me because of my injury, my wound is incurable! Yet I said this is my sickness, and I must endure."* Woe to you who think your pain is incurable; your pain is your sickness. If you say something it's yours; you claim that there's nothing that can be done to it without your permission. Let me remind you God didn't create slaves to pain and troubles; you don't have to claim ownership over them. They are not yours they are just the results of sin and man existed before sin. These men of leprosy their wound was incurable but they refused to be excluded because of the thing they themselves couldn't change. You can't change the past so why dwelling on them. I'm saying this because we are hurt by the past most of the time not the future. And because we are still in the past we can't enjoy the privileges of the present, and we can't plan our future. Realize when your time for weeping is over. How long will you carry that pain? Let it go ; it has served it's purpose and it is the burden not worth carrying. Everything has got time under the sun, and once it's over let it be. Move out of the night enjoy the privileges that comes with morning.

Some of us our time in pain has long expired but we are still hanging there. We don't even attempt talking about the pain because we are still nursing it so that we never forgive. We are waiting for the right time to get our sweet revenge. The expired thing is not enjoyable hence the bible give this warning to those who have stayed in pain for more than they were supposed to, *"gather up your belongings to leave the land, you who live under siege. For this is what the Lord says, at this time I will hurl out those who live in this land. I will bring distress on them so that they may be captured." Jer10:17-18*

You have over stayed your welcome in the place of siege. It's now time to move out, because the Lord will hurl out those who live in it. Why will he hurl them out? Because pain is admirable on its time, but it is very annoying when a person cannot move out on it in a long run. Such a person will find himself being distressed, soon depression will come to add on that leaving him sick. That's why when a person has been hurt for a long time he ends up being insane. Most of the people who are insane is due to the fact that they where hurt more than they could handle and it disturbed them to a point of insanity. Some try to quench it with alcohol and drugs but thus create a vicious cycle. Forgive and forget, that's all you need to do in dealing with pain. Remind yourself that life goes on and for it to go on it depends on your willingness. Know when it is over.

Let's go back a little to 2king7:3-4. Once these men with leprosy decided to move out of their siege they wasted no time. They moved within the twinkle of an eye to the camp of the Arameans. They did what the Lord has instructed on Jer10:1 and because they did the right thing God was with them, and he caused the Arameans to flee before them thinking that they were attacked by the great army. The Lord has helped the four men with leprosy; he can also help you. If there is one decision you need to make, that decision will be to move on and never stuck on one place.

Sorrow is not the permanent stay in our lives, it just sweep a way for the coming joy.

An incurable pain brings hatred towards certain things or people.

"*Her brother Absalom said to her, has Amnon your brother been with you? Be quite my sister, he is your brother don't take this thing to heart, and Tamar lived in her brother's house, as a desolate woman. Absalom never said a word to Amnon, either good or bad; he hated Amnon because he had disgraced his sister Tamar."2Sam13:1*

The bible says in the course of time, Amnon son of David fell in love with Tamar, the beautiful sister of Absalom son of David as well. Amnon became confused with the love he had for his sister to a point of being sick. His sister Tamar was still a virgin and it seemed impossible for Amnon to do anything to her. Amnon got advice from his friend Jonadam who suggested him to lie down and pretend to be sick, and ask Tamar to bring him food. Amnon forced himself on Tamar and the bible says after that he hated her with an intense hatred. The bible says he hated her more than he loved her. If we remember, he loved her to a point of sickness which means he now hated her to a point of death. He called his personal servant to chase her out of his house for he wanted nothing to do with her; he never wanted to see her again. Her brother Absalom accommodated her in his house. Now I want you to look carefully at what Absalom did here. He was deeply hurt by what Amnon did to his sister, but he pretended to be fine with it. He advised Tamar to keep quiet and never take the matter to heart while he himself was furious to a point of killing. Instead of searching help for Tamar he kept her on his house knowing that seeing her devastated brakes his heart. Absalom was secretly searching a way to revenge his sister to Amnon and he worked towards finding it patiently. It took him two years before he can find a way to make Amnon pay for what he has done. Imagine carrying hatred for the whole two years. How possible is that? To some people it is very possible they can even go beyond two years with their burden of hatred. I wonder how they cope with it. These people; like Absalom they know they are hurt but they keep quiet, they try by all means to hide the pain. When they meet with the person who has inflicted them with pain they pretend to be laughing while they grim. Even when pain devours them to a point of death they don't shout for help. Instead of moving on they are busy deriving ways to bring their enemies down. They laugh but at the back of their mind they can't wait for their revenge.

It is not good to bottle up, because things that are bottle up once they want to be visible they erupt living the place desolated. Stop pretending as if things don't mean a big deal whereas they do, because by doing so you are nursing and nourishing pain to grow and turn you into a monster. Stop torturing yourself; you have suffered enough from outside you don't need another torture from yourself. You are not a robot; you are a being with emotions. You have the right to feel pain and the responsibility of letting go, and you must forgive those who caused you pain(for your sake). Remember every right goes along with a responsibility. If there is a right to education the responsibility will be making education accessible to everyone. A right without its responsibility it's no longer a right but neglect. Use your rights wise with their responsibilities. Revenge is for God, Rom12:19

Deal with pain in time; avoid being like Absalom who cherished it until he killed his brother. Pro6:27 ask this question, *"can man scoop fire into his lap without his clothes being burned? Can man walk on hot coals without his feet being scorched?"*

A person who refuse to let go of pain is like the one who scoop fire on his lab thinking that he won't burn his clothes and the one who refuse to forgive is like the one who walks on hot coals with his bare feet. You might say Nonhlanhla doesn't know the pain I feel. Yes I might not know the pain you feel but I know the harm it will cause you; I know that it will keep you on halt as long as you are carrying it. Forgive and move on with your life.

When pain strikes we feel abandoned.

"From the sixth hour until the ninth hour darkness came over all the land. About the ninth hour Jesus cried out in a loud voice, "Eloi, Eloi lama sabachthani? Which means, "my God, my God why have you forsaken me? Matt27:45

Sometimes when pain strikes we feel forsaken not only by people but by God as well. The agony of pain makes us forget that God will never leave us. When we look on the people who things seem to go well for them we tend to think that God does not see us or has forgotten about us. It is absolutely not true, we are all his images how can he forget us? He won't; not for a moment. Now the question will be why some people experience terrible situation while others don't. When you read the newspaper you hear another story of rape after another, when you open a television you hear a criminal proclaiming his tenth victim. We are living in a fallen world where man went in search for the impurity. There are things that God can never control, like human beings. He gave them the power to choose. They can choose whatever they want it's in their control. But there are some cases where God will deliberately grieve us in order to search what is on our mind, Deu8:1, Job. In other cases he tests us to show us that he is with us every step we take. He wants to have a personal relationship with us to a point where we will acknowledge His value in our lives. Most of the time afflictions bring us closer to him, because when we are afflicted we pray more than when we are not. Even those who never pray begin praying in times of afflictions. Hence the bible says in Isaiah, "*I live on a high and holy place, but also with the contrite and lowly spirit, to revive the spirit of the lowly and the heart of the contrite.*" The contrite heart is the noisiest heart. It doesn't stop crying unto the Lord. It stands on the Lord until he shows mercy. God will never ignore such a heart.

In the mist of your sorrows never doubt the presence of God. He has guaranteed that he is with you in all of your troubles. He said, "I live". This statement shows the Lord's commitment to us. Something that you live with you cannot leave or forget it because since it is part of you it always has its place on your mind and heart, and it will always know where to find you. You are mindful of it to an extent that you won't do anything without considering it. Same applies to the Lord it is a sure case that he is with us in the midst of our problems. Another thing that will give us assurance that the Lord is always with us is because he is not the son of man that he should lie, whatever he promises he does. Allow him to revive your heart and spirit.

Jesus knew his mission on earth was to become a sin sacrifice and redeem the world. All this time when he was busy healing the sick and preaching the kingdom of God to people he knew that the hour will come for him to die on the cross, but he was never worried. He so many times told his disciples that he will be crucified but he never cared much about it; for he knew it was the Lord's will to suffer him. Now the time came for his predictions to come true, then he doubted the presence of the Lord. The agony of death made him feel as though he were alone. He was beaten, tortured, scoffed and his clothes were stripped off. He was humiliated so much but he never complained to the Lord, Then came the hour of darkness, Jesus who has done so well from the beginning of the road felt the absence of the Lord.

It will not always be easy in our lives, there are things that we can endure and the things that we can't. Those we can endure we must thank God for giving us the ability to carry them, and those we can't, like Jesus, we must confess to Him that we feel alone and abandoned. He will surely give us strength to carry on. Jesus has always relied on God, we saw him praying every time. Prayer was his everyday life because he knew that there are things that he couldn't do on his own. Remember he was fully human and fully God, so his human nature made him rely on prayer. We can also be like him; there's is nothing that is preventing us from living a prayerful life. Darkness comes to everyone's life; if it came to Jesus who was fully God and fully human being what will prevent it from coming to you. What I'm actually saying is, we should never despair in times of darkness. When the lights turn off in our lives it does mean God is blind. Eliphaz was once amused by Job's attitude then he said, *"think of how you have instructed many, how you have strengthened feeble hands. Your words have supported those who stumble; you have strengthened the faltering knees. But now trouble comes to you; you are discouraged; it strikes you; you are dismayed." Job 4:3-5.* The scripture above illustrate that Job had spent most of his time with the weak and those who are in pain encouraging them. He gave hope to the hopeless, but when trouble came to him he was discouraged. He wished as if life could not be given for those who are in misery, and life to the bitter soul, to those who long for death that does not come. It was hard for Eliphaz to believe that those words came out of Job who was the tower of strength to many. We are all human beings with flesh and blood and darkness comes to us all irrespective of the good we do.

Let's go back to Jesus; He has instructed his disciples not to be dismayed when the world hates them, John15:18-26 & 16:1-4. He has also told them that they will scatter and leave him alone; yet he is not alone for God is with him, Jonh16:31. This was before the cross/the hour of darkness, but when that hour came the very same Jesus who said my father is with me we hear him crying: "my father, my father why have you forsaken me." As I said that Jesus was fully divine as a son of God and fully man; at cross when he cried he was revealing the character of man. As God he can never cry but as a human being he can and he can also accuse God of forsaking him. From the story of Job and Jesus we learn that pain can make you feel forsaken even when you yourself know exactly that you are not forsaken. God is not like these parents of today who lack responsibility and abandon their children. In all circumstances he says fear not, for I have redeemed you, I have summoned you by a name, you are mine. When you pass through waters I will be with you, when you pass through rivers they will not sweep over you. *When you walk through the fire, you will not be burned; the flames will not set you blaze. IS 43:1-2*

God himself doesn't promise a life without fire but he promises that we will not be burned. Now the question is, how can fire not burn us? If God says it won't then it won't because he knows that he will protect us from it. He doesn't promise a life without rivers, but he promises that we will pass through without them sweeping on us. Believe and move without asking questions that leads to doubts. When I say stop asking questions I remember the officer in the book of 2king7:2 whom when the man of God said, *"by this time tomorrow the sear of fine flour will sell for a shekel and two sears of barley for a shekel at the gate of Samaria"*, he answered by saying, *"if the Lord could open the windows of heaven could this be?" The man of God said to him in fact you shall see it with your eyes, but you shall not eat of it."* You see what happen when we doubt God; we become spectators and testify about things that God does for other people but we never experience them.

He promised to be with you every step of the way. Don't

doubt him for he is faithful to all his promises.
Heb10:23
He will never lie or repent. Num23:19
God loves you the most, you are the work of art he beat his chest when looking at.

CHAPTER 5

Tests reveals the hidden thoughts of a person.

If God is there why have I gone through so much pain? This is the question most asked by people who have experienced so many trials and tribulations in their lives. Some of us have never experienced those tribulations but we still struggle with that question in our minds. The circumstances around us force us to doubt the existence of the loving God. Why? Because if my neighbor has no food; It affects me, once my brother is infected by HIV; I become affected. In no way I can enjoy my peace while others are suffering. When opening a newspaper you read another story after another about rape and murder, when you open a television you see stories about people who are starving to death, nations fighting against one another and diseases that are without a cure. So how do you believe God's love in circumstances like this? You tend to ask that if he loves and have compassion why he keeps quiet while others are being abused. Why doesn't he say a thing about those starving countries? And what about the diseases that kill people from day to day? These are some of the questions that God has to deal with on the daily bases.

Let's go back to Gen1, 2 & 3; when God formed man out of the dust of the earth, Everything was perfect and there were no horrible things like the ones I have mentioned. Man was given power to rule the earth; in fact he was god with small g. Until he himself decided to step low on his position of being a ruler and became a slave of the earth. He now had to toil before he can eat, and the earth produced thorn and thistles for him. Man sold with the authority that God gave him and everything became a great mess. All the bad and malicious things entered and ruled the earth because the one who was given dominion to rule lost it. Adam lost his power of dominion and it fell in the wrong hands of the one who wouldn't spare the world (Devil). We are not his image so whatever we go through he doesn't feel any pain because he has got nothing to lose. He uses us against God, he wants to tease him and say, "look at your images, look at yourself, is that really you? That rapist and murderer is that how you behave? These all sufferings are the results of Adam's disobedience.

Someone might say I hear what you are saying, but isn't God the omnipresent God? If he is; why didn't he rebuke Adam before he can taste the forbidden fruit? God can tell us good from wrong but he can't prevent us from taking wrong decision. If he were to prevent us there would have been no need for him to grant us choice; he could have easily controlled us, and if he were to control us this would have been contradictory to what he said when he created man. He said he is creating his image and likeness. He is a free God not controlled by anything hence he made us not to be controlled. Adam chose to disobey and he is the one who invited all this sorrows we are experiencing today." *Therefore, just as sin entered the world through one man, death entered through sin and this way death came to all men because all sinned. Rom 5:12*

There is no one righteous, not even one, all have sinned. What about that new born baby, has he also sinned? *Psalm51:5 say, "I was sinful at birth, sinful from the time my mother conceived me."* Sin separated us with the love of God. Instead of feeling the tender of his love we feel the coldness of the cruel sin. Psalm 51:5 tells us that no one is immune to sin. If we are sinful from the time we are conceived which means no one will escape the consequences of sin. Every time we suffer God wants to reach out and help us, but he is repelled by the wall of sin surrounding us, Is59:1-2. We are his image; when we suffer he suffers in silent that only if these people knew the life I intended when I created them. And it is very painful to him because he has the power to help us but he can't because we don't allow him to; we don't remove the wall of sin that surrounded us.

Why are we punished for Adam's sin? We are his seed and as long as we don't repent and accept Jesus as the savior of our lives we will continue to live in his curse. Jesus cleanses our sin and brings us to the life God want us to live. He makes pure and establish our friendship with God again.

What happens when we don't have Jesus in our lives? God doesn't have anything to do with us, because we don't have the mark which is Jesus blood that shows we are now adopted by God. When we pray our prayers will not be answered because sometimes we need God to help us but we are still hiding sin in us. For example, some need God to help him succeed in his studies yet he is happy to see his fellow failing mathematics. When we've got Jesus in our lives we know the right ways of asking from God because the Holy Spirit teaches us. When asking from God we should first cleanse ourselves; most especially our hearts because they contain all sorts of impurities. Some of us need God's help but we don't comply with his rules. Who do we think we are to control God? Remove the mark of sin that you have from birth by accepting Jesus as your Lord and savior. The Lord will not attend prayers of sinners read psalm66:16-20. This scripture teaches us how to pray and come near God.

Will my troubles end if I repent?
The answer to the above question is a big resounding YES dear. When you repent and accept Jesus as your Lord and Savior your troubles are substituted with tests. You no longer suffer from troubles but you enjoy the privilege of being tested by God. Troubles lead to suffering and pain, but test develop you into and stronger person. Too good to be true, isn't it? Let us take an example, those who are far from God; God allow them to be troubled so that they come close to him, Psalm119:67-71, 107:4-34. If it is always well for us we won't recognize the need of God in our lives. The bible say in Provebs19:3, *"A man's folly ruins his life, yet his heart ranges against the Lord."* It is foolish for one to carry on with his life as though God doesn't exist, Psalm14:1-4. God doesn't like foolishness because in his creation he didn't create fools, but man with wisdom to rule over everything.

God loves us all; that's why his sun shines upon us all, the only thing he hates is this sin that we love much. Let's explore Psalm107:10-12 a little, *"some sat on the darkness and deepest gloom, prisoners suffering in iron chains, for they had rebelled against the words of God and despised the counsel of the most high. So he subjected them to bitter labor, they stumbled, and there was no one to help."* Where was God if there was no one to help? He was right there watching and waiting for them to acknowledge that he can help them. Didn't he see them? Of course he did, they had rebelled against him so they had to suffer in order to come to their senses. We have our physical parents who discipline us when we disobey. Does that mean they hate us? No, it shows that they love us and don't want us to go astray because they know the dangers of doing so. They can't bear seeing us digging our own graves while they still need us to live. When talking about parents it reminds me of father's love. They are very harsh to such an extent that you will think that they hate kids. They can be very hard at times to their own children, but it doesn't mean they hate them. By being hard they train children to say no to bad things and cling to the ones that will make them proud. They turn us into men and women of good morals who can stand their grounds no matter what. If our physical parents who have no single idea of how we were created disciplines us when doing wrong how much more would the one who knows how our bones were joined together to form a structure? Discipline is the act of love and will never come easy because it cures the madness that we are most often not aware of. It must be so hard so that when thinking of straying again you hold yourself without any second thought. Whoever is wise let him heed this and consider the great love of God. It is because of the love that he has for us that he won't let us wander from his righteous ways. If you are wise heed these things that the Lord has done in Psalm 107 and know that he won't let you off the hook until you repent. Consider his love for you and start living a righteous life. In all your sorrows he is there waiting for you to call on him. He will do whatever it takes for you to acknowledge his love. You have always done that for the ones you love; whatever it took you sacrificed and fought teeth and nails with those who stood between you and them.

Tests reveal people's loyalty.
I said God allows troubles on those who are far from him to catch and bring them close to him, now let's see the difference between troubles and tests but this time we focus more on the tests. I said people who are in Christ are no longer suffering from troubles but God test them regularly. Why does he test them, isn't enough that they left behind all sin that the sons of men are enjoying? God tests them to see what is in their heart? A heart is deceitful above all things and beyond cure, from time to time God need to test this heart in order to know its plans and that it will pursue righteousness under all circumstances, and that it will continue loving him through all conditions of life.

"Remember how the Lord your God led you all the way in the desert these forty years, to humble you and to test you; in order to know what was in your heart whether or not you would keep his commandments." Det8:2

Tests reveal the hidden thoughts of the heart. If you want to see how reliable your friend is, go through certain tests then you will be sure of his loyalty. If he sticks with you know that he is a noble friend. Job's wife encouraged him to curse God and die when Job was tested. You can ask yourself what she wanted to do after Job's death. The test revealed that Job's wife loved

Job only when life was full of candies but once those candies were snatched away she grew tired of him. Life was good when Job was healthy but now that he was sick she wanted him to vanish; she couldn't stand him any longer. Throughout the book of Job she never appears, it was only Job and his friend questioning and answering one another I wonder where was she, doing what?

Simon Peter said these words to Jesus, "even if all fall away on account of you, I never will", Matt20:33. He also promised to die with him, he said, "*Lord I am ready to go with you to prison and to death, Luke22:33.*" Wait until death approached, he "Peter" ran away and followed from a distance, that wasn't enough he went farther and denied knowing him. Not once or twice but three times. To convince them that he wasn't familiar with what they were talking about he called curses on him and swore to them that he doesn't know Jesus. Immediately the cock crowed to remind him the words of Jesus when he said before the cock crow you would have denied me three times, Mark14:71. Even when the cock crowed Peter didn't immediately remember, for him to remember Jesus had to turn and look at him. I wonder how those eyes were when looking at Peter. Were they filled with disappointment, fear or awe? I wonder what was in those eyes that reminded Peter his promise.

There are things in our heart that we won't be aware of until we are tested. Job's wife didn't know that there will be a day where she will wish for his husband's death. Even Peter didn't know that he can deny the son of man. God test us to bring the subconscious mind to light.

Sometimes we are tested to realize how unreliable we can be or the people surrounding us. We have seen it happening to Job's wife and Peter. It is very dangerous to walk with people whom you don't know what's in their heart. They might turn against you while journeying, hence God tested the Israelites and he is now testing us, Ex13:17. We can't test ourselves, right! And it is most unlikely that we can test other people and come with best results, because people are good pretenders, so the test from God reveals the hidden character once and for all. God knows how to test the sincerity of our hearts by comparing it with the earnestness of others, and he can also test us to prove our love for him. Remember what the devil said when he and God were discussing about Job. *"Does Job fear you for nothing? Have not you put a hedge around him and his house hold, and everything he has? You have blessed the work of his hands; so that his herds and flocks are spread throughout the land." Job1:9*

The Lord God had to prove to the devil that Job will continue loving and being faithful to him after he had lost all he possessed. He allowed the devil to stuck down all Job had including his children; he even inflicted him with painful boils from head to the sole of his foot. Job didn't fail God by charging him wrong doing; instead he tore his robe, shaved his head, fell-down on the ground and worshiped the Lord. I wonder how you were going to respond to the situation had you been the one in Job's shoes. Some curse him if it has been raining for the whole week and they can't manage to go to work. Some curse him if they lack food for a day. In this life time no one is worthy to step into Job's shoes, even the LORD himself will not attempt testing us the way he tested Job.

Abraham had no children with his beloved wife Sarah. Abraham trusted on the LORD that someday he will bless him with an adorable child of his own. Once the child was born God tested him and ordered him to sacrifice the only son he has waited patiently for. God wanted to check whether Abraham's love will still be the same for him after he has got what he wanted. He didn't test him with something far from his heart but with the very close one. Abraham like Job didn't fail God. Why are you failing him? So far you are not the first person to be tested the way you are right now, nor will you be the last. I have given you the examples of people who refused to fail God, be like them; irrespective of tough situations, irrespective of how many are deserting you. Let go of those who want to leave and never focus on them, it shows that they were not destined to be with you. Abraham waited for years for his son Isaac to be born and when God said give him back to me he didn't hesitate even for a moment. He knew that if he has given him (Isaac) at the age of 99 he can manage to give him another child again. If the Lord has brought you this far he can also carry you forward. If he has supplied for today's bread he will supply even for tomorrow's bread as well.

We must not place our hearts on things that God blessed us with, because if he has blessed us nothing will withhold hold him from taking them "when he wants". If he blesses you with a good paying job don't close your eyes to those who are in need. You are not in that work for yourself but to serve the Almighty God with it. And always tell yourself that if God has given you something good it is well and he decides to take it back it still okay.

When Jephthah was about to fight on behalf of Israel with the children of Ammon he made a vow to the Lord that if he can deliver his advances into his hands; then it will be whatever that comes out of the doors of his house to meet him will be of the Lord. Guess who came to meet Jephthah! His lovely daughter, and because he has given his word to God he couldn't reverse it. He had to be faithful to his vow that he made before God. Again; our honesty is not tested like Jephthah whereby we will have to take the lives of our daughters by our own hands. Our tests are far better than the way the ancient believers were tested. If you were Jephthah I guess you would have said no God not this one. I didn't know it was her who would come to meet me. You were now going to be like Peter who acted against his words. We still have Peters to this day, some are even worse than him because they don't regret. After Peter has denied Jesus he wept in regret, but those of today they carry on with their lives as though nothing has happened. When you turn to look at them with a disappointed face they don't even blush as long as they are covered and save.

Tests are good for equipping us with knowledge.

"These are the nations that the Lord left to test all the

Israelites who had not experienced any of the wars in Canaan (He did this only to teach warfare to the decedents of the Israelites who not had previous battle experience). We have spoken about the tests whereby God wants to test people's loyalty; now is time we speak about test where God's want to equip us with knowledge. The scripture above speaks about the nation that the Lord had left in order to train the Israelites who had no previous experience in battle. How awesome is that. God doesn't what us to remain childish so he tests us with difficulties to allow growing take place in us, increase our intelligence and knowledge. He wants us to acquire knowledge on how to solve problems, that's why you will find that you are a born again Christian but still you swim in a pool of tests that seem to turn into problems. When trying to fix this side the other one collapses, when you turn to this side nothing seem to do. You are at school to be equipped with the knowledge on how to solve problems and you need not to fail because children who fail disappoint teachers. You do not only get a lesson on how to solve problems but you will also get a qualification to be a teacher to those who will be struggling to keep up with their tests. You see, when you chose to fail; you are not the only one who will be failing but also the people who will come to you in future searching for answers. Never fail because by doing so you are playing with people's answers and risking their lives. Had Job failed his test; we also were going to fail because we were going to use him as an excuse to fail. We were going to say if Job who was trusted by God failed his test what will prevent me from doing the same. There are people who are already stationed in the place you are about to pass whom you will get answers from. Haven't you ask yourself sometimes why people like to share their problems with you? It is because God has inserted their answers in you, some of the answers are from the challenges you conquered along the journey.

My father died when I was seven years old, but even before his death he wasn't around most of the time. When I was doing grade 8 I needed him a lot. Most of the children were bragging a lot about their fathers and being the talkative as I am I had nothing to say. It was in times like this I started questioning God why did he take my father away from me. I enjoyed writing poems and in these poems I would express myself by writing my feelings down. I wanted to make the pain vanish but I didn't know how. I crowded myself with a group of boys to quench the need of being around my dad, but it never helped. I looked on several dads to get the picture of how my dad would be like, but they were not good fathers; in fact they made me hate fathers because they were not good to their own children. Today when I meet with children whom are going through the same situation I went through I am able to help them. I tell them how I have conquered the situation, and how I have broken the habit of being crowded by males.

Had Jesus failed the test of dying on the cross he would have failed God and the whole world. There was a time where he wished the cup can be taken away from him, Luke 22:42. Like Jesus we sometimes wish as if the cup we are drinking from can be taken away. The question is if we don't want to drink off our cup; who else would drink from it? I like Jesus' prayer, though he wished for the cup to be taken away from him he remembered the

Lord's will, he said nevertheless not my will but yours be done. So we might not like the things that are happening in our lives but the Lord's will need to fulfill its purpose in our lives. No matter our feelings, God's will come first and therefore it must be honored in our lives. Jesus prayed for the Lord to take away the cup from him, let's see how the Lord answered him. *"And the angels from God appeared and strengthen him."* Here we are expecting to hear the answer of the Lord as to whether he is willing to remove the cup or not, but we see the angel coming to strength him. What is this suppose to mean? Prayer gives power. In every trial we meet God has already provided power for us to make it through; yet such power is found only in prayer. If we don't pray we will always struggle with things we can easily conquer. Some of our answers are inserted within our prayers; all we need to do is to pray continuously without being discouraged. God's will require us to finish and pass the given tests. He had no use of truant who will come back blundering to him with work half done. Don't pray for God to remove your challenges but pray him to give you strength to defeat and pass through challenges. Go into the other side of the challenge and get out at the other side, you see how simple is it? When you get through the other side you get in weak and without knowledge, but once you make it and come out at the other side; you come out equipped with knowledge and stronger than ever. Whatever challenge that comes your way face it head up and collide with it head on for you've got power to defeat.

When tested rejoice.

"Consider it pure joy, my brothers whenever you face many trials of many kinds, because you know that the testing of your faith develops perseverance. Perseverance must finish its work so that you may be mature, and complete; not lacking anything." James 1:2-4

What does this scripture imply? It implies that you must not pray for life without trials for you will not mature. If you are not tested ask God to test you, but I don't believe there is a person who is not tested. God wants us to develop perseverance so that it complete its work within us, leaving us not lacking anything. Life without tests denies us the opportunity to know the other side of God. Therefore I encourage being of Paul's character who rejoiced in weakness, insults, hardships, persecutions, and difficulties for Christ's work to be revealed in him. You also must delight yourself in sorrows to see God's splendor.

Don't look for short cuts to come out of your test.

"He slept with Hagar and she conceived. When she knew she was pregnant, she began to despise her mistress. Then Sarai said to Abraham, "you are responsible for the wrong I am suffering. I put my servant in your arms, and now that she knows she is pregnant she despises me. May the Lord judge between you and me." You servant is in your hands, Abraham answered, do to her whatever you think is best. Sarai began ill treated Hagar; so she fled from her." Gen 16:4-6

Sarah tested herself by giving her servant to her husband. She had borne Abraham no children, so she gave Hagar to Abraham to sleep with thinking that perhaps she can build a family through her. She wanted to help God on fixing her problem of not getting children. Let me advice you; no matter what the circumstance may be don't try to help God, By doing so you will be inviting problems that you won't be able to deal with in the near future. Once Hagar learned that she was pregnant, she began despising Sarah. She thought she was her equal because they were now sharing the husband. Sarah created a vicious circle while trying to look for a short cut out of her test. That's what most of us end up doing when tested. Provebs14:12 give this advice, *'there is the way that seem right to man, but its end is the way of death."* By giving Hagar to her husband Sarah shot herself on the leg thinking that she will be off the hook. Always when given a test chose a godly way out of it, irrespective of how long it will take for you to reach the end.

Don't forget your position for you will be making things more difficult for yourself.
Hagar forgot that she was only the servant in Abraham's house. Her pregnancy was not changing a thing. Though she carried Abraham's first son/heir the roof she stayed under still belonged to Sarah and that gave her the right to do anything she wanted with her at any time. This scripture warns us to stay a mile away from married men because they use us only for their pleasure, but once things back fires they run back to their wives. They dish you out like hot potatoes and you will be left alone to suffer the consequences. While you enjoy each others' company they treat you like a queen so that you don't

run away, but wait until things get hot they get rid of you as fast as they can. If you are not married wait for God to bless you with your husband in his own time. Stop blessing yourself with the one who already has a family. I know that it is good to love and be loved, but a married man play a mile away from him.

The manner in which Hagar despised Sarah; Sarah was forced to fight back. She ill treated her to a point whereby she couldn't stand it any longer. The bible said she fled. She kindled fire now that it was burning she couldn't stand it. Don't start what you won't finish. The medicine that you cook you must be prepared to drink and finish yourself. Had Hagar remained on her position of being a servant even though she was pregnant with her master's son there wouldn't be any reason for her to flee? Now the question is where is our position in times of tests? Our position is in prayer and worship. Tests must not keep us away from God but closer to him. Hagar on her way met with the angel of the Lord that told her to go back and submit to her mistress. Here we are taught not to run away from our problems because since they are part of us they will always know where to find us. The angel advice Hagar to go back and fix the damage she has caused. I repeat it once again; don't look for short cuts out of your tests. If you are not married stay unmarried until the Lord decide it is time for you to get married. If you are unemployed don't steal from those who work. Wait in prayer.

In the book of 2Cor7:10 Paul wrote these words, "Godly *sorrow brings repentance that leads to salvation and leaves no regret, but worldly sorrow brings death."* Godly sorrows are from God and he sends them in order to produce the good out on us, and worldly sorrows are the ones we ourselves go in search for them. They live us hurt and in unending regrets, they can even lead to death. When I talk about death I don't only talk about the kind of death where a person will go to the grave. I'm referring to the kind of death where your dreams and ego will be affected. It is very hard to move with a wound and those who manage are very few and some remain living corpses. Avoid committing suicide.

Chapter 6

Challenge the situations with the word of God.

"Elijah was afraid and ran for his life. When he came to Beersheba in Judah, he left his servant there, while he himself went a day's journey into the desert. He came to a broom tree, sat down under it and prayed that he might die.

"I am no better than my ancestors." 1Kings 19:3-4

Elijah was the prophet of God in the time of king Ahab's reign who was married to a dangerous woman, "Jezebel." Jezebel was notorious of killing the Lord's prophets and worshiping Baal. Elijah stepped on her toe by killing 450 prophets of Baal so she wanted to avenge them. She sent a word to Elijah that he also will follow the prophets of Baal. Elijah who had witnessed many miracles of God was now terrified by the woman. He was feed by the ravens (1kings 18:4-6); he returned from the dead the son of the widow from Zarephth (kings19:23); he once was carried by the holly spirit of God (1kings18:40); he once called fire of the Lord to burn the sacrifice (1king18:36-38), and he had killed 450 prophets of Baal (1kings18:40). Now one word from Jezebel was enough to make him forget all those experiences and made him consider himself same as his ancestors. One word from Jezebel made him forget the Lord whom he is serving and flee for his life. The funny part of it is that he was running so that Jezebel doesn't kill him but he ended up praying for death. None of his ancestors have experienced all that he has experience with the Lord but he considers himself to be like them. This shows that we should never; never be controlled by fear because it captures our memory so that we don't stand for what we believe in. Elijah prayed in a way I don't wish any one of us to, *"take my life Lord."* David was once chased by Saul and Absalom in pursuit for his life but he never prayed such a prayer. So don't pray for God to take your life rather pray him to give you strength to continue until the end of the road. After this prayer Elijah felt asleep.

Too long is the journey of life. Many times we stop traveling and ask ourselves, when is it going to end? When trying to rebuild this side the other collapses leaving us dismayed. Elijah was re-establishing the relationship between God and Israel, but on doing that he angered Jezebel who couldn't wait to kill him. Sometimes we find ourselves in the situation like Elijah's; where we have to stand our grounds as individuals. He was the only one prophet of the Lord left from those whom Jezebel killed; or he wasn't aware that there are still others that the Lord have hid. He was there alone with no one to stand with, but God. I like what he did; he didn't say the majority is right. That's what kills us most of the time, "the majority is right". What if they are wrong? Or they will still be right on their wrong. Stand your ground even if there's no one to support you. If you don't have supporters know that you don't need them if you were going to need them God will have provided some for you. And stop wishing for your death to come because things don't work out for you. When that thought comes to your mind just take a quick look around, you will see that you are far better than the people surrounding you. Some lack food, some are sick and there's no cure for their diseases. I can fill this book if I was to discuss about challenges that people meet on their daily life and still they don't wish to die. They just take one day at a time. By this I was just saying keep moving no matter the circumstances.

While sleeping the angel of the Lord woke him and gave him food. He drank and ate and lay down again. The angel of the Lord came back for the second time and touched him and said, *"Get up and eat for the journey is too much for you."* After eating Elijah got his energy back; he traveled for forty days and nights until he reached Horeb, the mountain of the Lord. The lesson we take here is that even when we fall we wake again. Those who don't wake are those who don't listen to the angel waking them. By the time we are down we need to eat and consume all we can so that when we wake up like Elijah we walk without getting tired. What must we eat? We must eat the word of God. The word of God has all the answers you need and it can also provide you with hope and energy. Don't die while you've got the answers right at hand. Elijah only needed food from God not from anyone else. You likewise, when the going gets tough you need spiritual food which is, "God's word". It will strengthen and encourage you. Now look back to your life and view all the battles you have lost, wasn't it because you didn't read the bible? All scripture is God breathed and useful for teaching, rebuking, correcting and training righteousness, so that the man of God will thoroughly be equipped for every good work. When we don't read the word of God terrible situation finds us off guard and we will not deal with them accordingly because we are not taught and equipped for every challenge. God's word has the unlimited power that you can't understand, his word it is him, Jonh1:1. Please don't despise the bible it helps. When you despise it you despise God himself and you are never blameless before him.

People are perishing because of lack of knowledge.

"See my people are destroyed from lack of knowledge." Ho4:6

The challenges crush us because we lack knowledge and we are very ignorant. We are going about so much looking for answers in wrong directions while the bible is there waiting for us to open and read it. Once you open it you will feel God comforting you and easing all you anxiousness. The troubles you thought are bigger than you; you will start seeing them as small as an ant, because greater is he who is within us than what seem to trouble us.

" Why do you go about so much changing your ways, you will be disappointed by Egypt as you were by Assyria; you will also leave that place with your hands covered head for the Lord has rejected those you trust, you will not be helped by them." Jeremiah2:36-37

When you read the word of God you will stop boring people with your problems. Even when you go to them it will not be on regular basis as though your life depends on their answers. Our God is a jealous God Exo20:5. Since he is jealous he wants you to depend completely on himself. Hence he rejects the people we trust so that we can put our trust on him. If we always depend on people for advices it turns into idolatry. We worship those people without being aware of it. You hear people saying I know if so and so was here things like these would never happen; it's a form of idolatry; so and so is not here start living. Something that God has rejected it won't work; no matter how much you trust on it. That's why sometimes the most trusted friend; those you pray with every day betray you. You tell them a secret once they step out of their houses the whole world knows about. You once told them, it remained a secret and you are surprised why this time they back stab you. It's because the Lord doesn't want that form of idolatry you are busy trying to form, he rejects them so that they disappoint you. Not that they really planned to disappoint you it just happens. I'm not implying that asking advices from people it's a sin. All I am saying is that; ensure it doesn't turn into a form of idolatry.

The bible will provide you with best ways to deal with your challenges. For instance if there is somebody disturbing your peace the bible says pray for the well being of that person because if he prospers you also will prosper. When your husband cheat on you, don't take the phone and swear at the ladies he cheats with just pray God to bless them with peaceful marriages so that they leave your husband to you. The bible says; *also seek the peace and the prosperity of the city to which I have carried you into exile, pray to the Lord for it, because if it prospers, you too will prosper, Jer29:7.* You see the difference: friends will advise you to beat the lady until she leaves your husband alone. What if she beat you or decides that she would rather die than leave your husband? Here the bible gives us a peaceful manner to solve our problems. You pray for her first and go and speak with her in your best manner bearing in mind that your happiness does not lie with you only but with those who persecute you as well; if they stop persecuting you your happiness will bliss.

The person who is equipped with the word of God knows how to handle problems better. When tragedy strikes he doesn't falter because he is already strengthened. *He knows that all his sighing lies open before the Lord, Psalm38:9.* He is not easily discouraged because he always stands upon the word. When darkness cloud his way he speaks the words of confidence that he will see the goodness of the Lord even in that darkness, Psalm27:13-14. Read the word of God and trust on it.

Practice what you read on the word.
Don't just read the word in order to correct people but practice it yourself; by not practicing the word you push other people to the right direction whereas you pursue your way to hell. People pay more attention to what you do more than to what you say. If I advise you about how to handle you finance you must see it first on me that really this person knows how to handles his finances. Paul said in 1 Cor9:27, *"no, I beat my body and make it my own slave so that after I have preached to others, I myself will not be disqualified for the prize."* When reading the word it must convert you before it can convert the surrounding. You are a moving bible those who refuse to read it will see its effects upon your life and will gradually change without even looking in it. It must first

begin with you; before preaching that sex before marriage it's a sin you must first stop doing it yourself. Before I preach about forgiveness I must first forgive those who offend me irrespective of how big the offense is. Hide the word in your heart so that you don't sin against God, Psalm119:11.

The word is not read only to solve our problems but also to correct our steps. Jeremiah said when praying; I know oh Lord that a man's life is not his own, it is not for man to direct his steps. If a man's life is not his own then whom do it belong to, and if it is not for man to direct his steps then who must direct him? God created man for his glory and he is the one who suppose to direct our steps. In the beginning God spoke with man face to face, latter he spoke with his people through his prophet and in this life time he speaks with us through the bible and the Holly spirit. He directs our steps through the bible, so if you have not started reading it you are missing out. When the bible says a man's life is not his own, it reminds us that nothing in this world belong to us. Starting with the flesh we carry; it belongs to the ground which is the Lord's. The spirit we have belongs to him as well. If I borrow you my car I expect to find it in its original condition. For me to ensure that I get my car in its original condition I must give rules concerning it. God has borrowed us his spirit and the time will come when he will collect it. Isn't a right thing that he finds it in its original state? Eze18:4 says, *"every soul belongs to me, the father and the son.* So in order to sustain "this borrowed spirit" you need to follow the bible's precaution. Live like a stranger in this world for the sake of your soul. The owner will not accept it once it is damage with the broken heart he will have to throw it in hell. It will no longer be worthy to dwell with him in his sanctuary.

"It is not for man to direct his steps." No matter how wise you may be but you cannot direct your steps, you need God to direct you. Teenager who think they are old enough to make their own decision they stumble and end in regrets. A person who thinks he is clever enough to direct his step without God leading him; if he doesn't suffer in this life time he will suffer in the coming life. On guiding their children parents need to depend on God's word so that they do not misguide them. On handling their marriage couples need to depend on God's word to guide them. When dealing with pain, anger, sadness, jealous, unforgiving, etc; one needs to depend on God's word to teach him best. You see! The word of God is the gem of life.

The bible is our code of conduct.

At work we have conventionalized set of principles or rules that we follow. We ensure that we do not omit them for there could be serious consequences that may follow. We obey those rules and warn others to do the same. Although we can have a code of conduct at work there is no accurate one like the bible. The work code of conduct applies only at work, once you leave the work premise the rules are dead, but the bible has no limit. It builds families with peace Eph5:22, it establish good relationship between masters and slaves Eph6:5-9, and it encourages children to respect their parents Eph6:1-4. There is no department where the bible doesn't fit; from children to parents, wives to husbands, slaves to masters, administrators and leaders they as well have their share in the bible. If this world was full of people who are reading the bible what would this planet be? We wouldn't cry about corruption in work areas, we wouldn't notice the imbalance between the haves and the non haves. We wouldn't cry so much about crime and disobedient children who lack decency.

Apply the word to any given situation.

"The hand of the Lord came upon me and brought me out in the spirit of the Lord and set me down in the mist of the valley and it was full of bones." Ezekiel 37

The truth is most of the time in our lives we find ourselves in tough situations where we will have to battle for change or our way out. We never invite these situations, but they come while we least expect them. You will agree with me when I say it's not about how many challenges you meet as an individual, but it's about how you tackle them. We don't go to the shelves of challenges and pick the one which we think we can best deal with; however we chose the manner in which to deal with them. Ezekiel was not really in the valley of dry bones, but here; dry bones are used to give a picture of people he was living among. They were like dry bones with their skins, flesh and muscles on. The reason that made them to appear like dry bones while they had flesh, muscles and skin is because they lacked hope. So if you are hopeless know that you are like a dry bone. (fly in)

"Then he caused me to pass by them all around and behold

there were very many in the open valley, and indeed they were very dry." inspect what is challenging you, pass by it all around and ensure that you know what you are facing. Sometimes we go through war without a thorough inspection and we lose because we under estimated the opponent or over estimated the opponent. Study your opponent very well and be sure of its condition; sometimes you will find that you are scared of a dry bone which is useless even to dogs, because if you can throw a very dry bone to the dog it will never eat. Once it has sniffed it; it will just pass by. Therefore when facing challenges never rush to fight or give up without a thorough inspection. Check all the side and see the best way to attack. Do it patiently and never quit before you see the side that you can attack on. While passing through the bone Ezekiel saw that they were very dry. What do you see when inspecting what you are facing right now? What are the weak points you notice about it? When David was facing Goliath he saw him too tall to be not missed with a sling. David was supposed to be terrified by Goliath's height, but he used it to his advantage.

"And he said to me, son of man can this bones live, so I answered, o Lord God, you know." After examining your opponent communicate with God about it. Give him all the details of what you see. Then he will ask a question that challenges your faith, can you defeat what you see? That's where the Israelites in the time of Goliath were defeated. That's where you and I are defeated. We are defeated by what we see before we can even attempt fighting. Why? Because we don't look at what we are

about to fight with faith but we look at it with fear, and fear always show us the opposite. Go back a little in your life; check all the battles you lost, you will agree with me when I say you didn't fail/lose because you tried all your level best and eventually lost. No! You assessed the situation (that is the very right thing to do), but when it came to communication with God you failed because you didn't believe. I love the story of David and Goliath very much it has a great lesson to teach. Saul studied well his opponent (Goliath); he even knew his history. There came a question that we all struggle to answer, can you fight what you see on the records? God doesn't care what the record says but he is looking for a person who can stand in the gap and prove the records wrong. If you say, you oh Lord knows, you give him the honor that is worth His greatness. You confess that there is where your knowledge ends and His is the great one, and there are things you can't fathom, but He alone can. God will give a way in which you can use to win the battle. Had Ezekiel answered according to the way he judged the situation he would have continued living with hopeless people for the rest of his life. Believe me when saying it is very annoying to leave with hopeless people, because they are all asleep and no one dare to wake one another.

"Again he said to me, prophesy to these bones and say to them O dry bones hear the word of the Lord." Ezekiel is now apply the word of God to the given situation. It didn't matter how very dry where they; for the fact that God spoke; the bones obeyed. The very same word Ezekiel used is the very same word which is right in

your hands, you can also apply it. Tell the problem that you don't care how impossible it might seem to remove it permanently, but the word of God say what is impossible to man it is not possible with God. It might come wearing the impossible but God says with Him it is possible. Tell the stress that is attacking you that you understand very well that the situations force you to worry but the word of God said, "I" should not worry about anything small or big, Matt6:25. Don't be afraid to speak with the difficulties using the word of God. Ezekiel spoke with dry bones to take shape, he instructed the breath of life to get through and it happened, which means everything has the ability to listen.

Check out!!!

You don't need to worry yourself about anything in life because you've got the one who cares so much about you. David said in Psalm23, *"the Lord is my shepherd; I shall not be in want"*, in ancient time the shepherd use to walk in front of the flock and the flock will follow from behind. When David says the Lord is his shepherd he tells us that the Lord is the one who is guiding him. He walks following the one who knows the way better and he trusts in his wisdom as the flock trust the shepherd's. A shepherd takes care and provides the needs of his flock, as a shepherd God also provide for our needs. Abraham testified that He is the provider (Jehovah Jireh). Our God doesn't change Malachi3:6, if he has provided for our father Abraham he can still provide for us.

"He makes me lie in green pastures", he makes us live in abundance, but the problem is, there are sheep that refuse to be led. They want to take their ways and expect the Lord to provide. It doesn't work like that. The shepherd feed the sheep that are with him. *"He leads me beside quiet water."* A shepherd doesn't allow the flock to drink water where they could easily drown. God will never lead you to a place where you will die and he will never let you dwell on the place where your safety is not guaranteed. He will also not lead you to a place where he knows he won't provide peace. Still we have the problem with the sheep that want to lead themselves and blame God when it back fires. He is Jehovah Shalom,

Shalom means peace.

"He restores my soul". Within the flock when there's a sheep that doesn't feel well the shepherd takes care of it and ensure that it is restored. He checks what could be the problem and take immediate steps to solve the problem. No matter how large the flock might be but he takes delight in one sheep as if it were alone Luke15:4-6. The Lord as our shepherd He knows our condition, and he can see when things are not going well with us. When our spirits are contrite and our hearts are broken he does not despise us Psalm51:17. He focuses his whole attention to us, revives our hearts and spirits and restores our souls Is57:15. He is Jehovah Ropher, the one who heals us. When our hearts are overwhelmed with sorrow and revenge he brings them back, because no shepherd will leave his flock lost. The only flocks that will be left to be lost are the ones with pride. The ones that thinks they know best than the shepherd.

"He guides me in the path of righteousness for his name sake." For the sake of His name the Lord will always guide us in the path of righteousness. He warned the Israelites not to misuse his name and He will not do anything that will make people criticize it. God is not like us whom we forbid people do certain things while we drive them into doing them. I don't want people to gossip about me but I do things that make them end up gossiping. If I don't like when people talks about me behind my back I must stop doing things that will make them talk. He is Jehovah Tsidkenue the Lord our righteousness.

"Even though I walk in the shadows of death I will fear no evil for you are with me." This shepherd goes with us through each and all circumstances of life. When we go through fire he is right there to ensure that we are not burned. When we go through water is with us to see to it that we are not swept over by the rivers. This encourages us to approach all conditions of life without fear for He is always there. He is Jehovah Shamma, the Lord who is there "Your rod and your staff comfort me." It is very scary to pass through fire and water but faith and hope makes it bearable. Have faith and hope that this shepherd will never give you over to death.

"You prepare the table before me in the presence of my enemies." After you have conquered the shadow of death he prepares the table not in secret but in the presence your enemies, those who were happy to watch while you were suffering and those who couldn't wait to see you dead. The other part of the enemies are the things which are within you that keep you from achieving. e.g pride and fear. By the time you are in the shadow of death you will let go of pride and trust in God, more over you will stop fearing. Once you have overcome pride and fear will watch you at the table. In difficulties do not quit until you reached the prepared table where you head will be anointed with oil and your tears wiped.

"My cup overflows." Whatever he is going to bless you with it will to overflow. "Your joy will equal the ocean. Surely love and goodness will follow me all the days of my life." You won't go around looking for goodness and to be loved for his goodness and love will be sufficient

for you all the days of your life. Once all these things are done you need to dwell in the house of the Lord. When it says the house of the Lord it talks about his presence. We are in his presence when we do his will, but when we go against it we go far from His presence.

Let be not a day that will pass without you reading the bible. Reading the bible is like training for battle. When going to war we train in advance, we don't wait until the ware has begun and say to the enemy let me fetch my sword and learn how to use it. Same applies to the bible; you don't search for scriptures when you are attacked but they must be right in your mind. When you have read them, in times of war the Holy Spirit will remind you, but if you didn't read He won't be able to remind you. Eph6:13 say put the full amour of God, so that when the day of evil comes, you stand your ground, and after you have done everything, to stand. Read from verse ten. A sheep doesn't fight for its-self for the shepherd does all the fighting on its behalf. It just stands firm until it is rescued by the shepherd, but the sheep that doesn't take rules will run all over the place in times of war until it is hurt. In times of struggles stand firm upon the word of God.
Finally; all has been said now the matter lies on your hands!!!

www.ingramcontent.com/pod-product-compliance
Lightning Source LLC
Chambersburg PA
CBHW071236090426
42736CB00014B/3111